A WHISPER IN THE WIND

CAN YOU HEAR ME NOW

DERRICK TURNER

A Whisper in the Wind
Copyright © 2022 by Derrick Turner

All rights reserved. No part of this publication may be reproduced, distributed, or transmitted in any form or by any means, including photocopying, recording, or other electronic or mechanical methods, without the prior written permission of the author, except in the case of brief quotations embodied in critical reviews and certain other non-commercial uses permitted by copyright law.

ISBN
978-1-957378-09-1 (Paperback)
978-1-957378-08-4 (eBook)

TABLE OF CONTENTS

Summary v
Acknowledgements.. vii

PART 1

Chapter 1 3
Chapter 2 9
Chapter 3 13
Chapter 4 17
Chapter 5 21
Chapter 6 25
Chapter 7 31

PART 2

Chapter 1 39
Chapter 2 41
Chapter 3 43
Chapter 4 47

Chapter 5 51
Chapter 6 55
Chapter 7 59
Chapter 8 63
Chapter 9 67
Chapter 10 73
Chapter 11 77
Chapter 12 81
Chapter 13 83
Chapter 14 85
Chapter 15 89
Chapter 16 93
Chapter 17 95
Chapter 18 97

PART 3

Chapter 1 101

SUMMARY

I was nineteen years old when I met the demon for the first time. The cunning and baffling of its character defects captivated me, and held me hostage for years. I became an addict whose life spiraled outta control! It was a monster, cleverly camouflaged in a puff of smoke I called, "the devil's love potion."

Trapped in a world of crushed dreams, false hope, and unmanageability, I was weakened and defeated by the intrusion of my new best friend. Blinded by the realities of my addition, I hit bottom over and over again.

I had gone completely insane, and at the brink of suicide, when a final cry to God brought me back from hell.

ACKNOWLEDGEMENTS

First, I would like to thank God who is the head of my life. Without him none of this would have been possible. A special thanks to those who continue to encourage me, as I tell my stories of trial and tribulation, to triumph and victory! I wanna give a special thanks to my devoted wife, Yvette Turner for her honesty about my work, and her constructive criticism. Thanks to my sister, Dorothy Coleman for her positive input in my life that paved the way over the years, and for all those times in the past when she thought I wasn't listening. Thanks to my niece, Erricka Coleman for her interests in these projects. And most importantly, my Mom and Dad for giving me life, and for teaching me how to be a man, despite the storms we endured.

A WHISPER IN THE WIND
"Can you hear me now"

The building was dark, cold and abandoned. It was made of red brick, and it stood three stories high. Every window had been broken out by the mischievous juveniles that roamed the streets getting in all sorts of trouble when they should've been in school. Every room of the building was littered with empty beers cans, food containers and bottles filled with urine that put out a grotess stinch that whipped through the air attacking my nostrils every time I inhaled. You could hear the pitty pat of rats, cats and stray dogs moving about the premises, marking their territory and searching for scraps of food left by junkies and addicts who had also made the dwelling their home. Empty crack bags, old cigarette lighters and burned spoons used to cook heroin, were scattered throughout the condemned building. It was a dark place that held a reputation for lost souls, broken dreams and crushed hope. Many had met their demise at the grip of addiction, chasing that next high, overdosing in need of feeling that first hit! The building was a hell above ground, a lonely place of despair and missed opportunities. Men and women met here daily, drowning their sorrows and guilt in a glass pipe or syringe. It was a horrifying vision of a place for the undead.

This was the east side of Chicago where a fraction of the city's wealthiest families resided. Beautiful homes and mansions stood with authority throughout the community. Golf courses were only a few feet away from the neighborhoods in any direction. The cool breeze of the nearby lakefront engulfed the air in the warm summer sun. It was like two worlds that separated themselves by a few city blocks. Two totally different lifestyles that passed one another, neither giving attention to the other.

I wasn't exactly lacking the knowledge of drugs, I had grown up in the midst of it in my own neighborhood. I had seen the destruction of addiction in my family, but I never understood how something could have so much control over one's life. The powdery white substance that transformed into the form of a rock, with the help of a little water and baking soda, baffled me. It was a mixture of chemical genius that gripped the will of many who dared to partake in its potion. It was the devil's love potion so cleverly disguised to have the answer to any problems I faced.

PART 1

CHAPTER 1

I WAS ABOUT 19 YEARS OLD when cocaine hit my neighborhood. All the older cats that schooled me were snorting it, injecting it and smoking it. It was the drug for the cool studs who portrayed themselves as players and pimps. The ones that wore the flashy gold chains and watches, and big gold nugget rings. The ones that drove the long cadillacs and flashed the huge bank roles of money, these were the guys I was fascinated by. They made using drugs seem like the coolest thing to do. I had no idea that it would ruin my life.

I was in my sophomore year in college when I smoked my first hit, I remember it like it was yesterday…..

I had just gotten my heart broken by the prettiest girl on campus, Nedra Johnson. We had been dating about a year when I found out the guy who was suppose to be her brother, was in fact, her fiance. The news was so devastating, it tore my heart in half, she was the first girl I'd been in love with. This guy was picking her up from school everyday, and I never noticed a thing. She made me look like a complete fool!

The word spread around campus like a wild forest fire, everybody knew. It had taken me two years to become the most popular guy on campus, but none of that meant nothing to me once my heart got broken, she had crushed me, and I needed something to fight the pain. I left the campus, and walked across the street to Grant Park. That was what I liked most about the school's location, it was downtown, and directly across the street from the park. I had my own little spot where I went when I needed to do some serious thinking. The weather was nice, and all I wanted to do was get as high as I could. I sat down in my little secluded spot, and rolled up a fat joint. I sat there for hours, smoking joint after joint, until my eyes were red as blood and almost completely closed. But, the weed wasn't helping my situation, the more I smoked, the more I thought about the break up. The high sent me into deep thought as the tears wet my face and flooded down my neck, drenching my shirt. The pit of my stomach balled up like two fists! I never knew being in love could hurt so bad, I was a total wreck!

My best friend had warned me about girls like Nedra, she was a perfect 10. She was five feet 4 inches tall, a smooth caramel complexion, small but, nicely shaped. Her hair jet black and silky, fell down the center of her back, complimenting her beautiful brown bedroom eyes. She was Brazilian, the finest girl on campus. I watched many men at school drool over Nedra, but she chose me. I guess I was getting what I deserved, I had broken some hearts myself to make room for her in my life, and now it was payback!

Finally, I pulled myself together and headed for the El-Train, I needed to get home and talk to someone about what I was feeling. The ride on the train seemed longer than usual, and it felt like everybody on the train was staring at me, sitting there looking like a close relative had just died. I sat by the window, staring into space, trying to understand my emotions. "Is this what love feels like," I thought to myself, "if it is, I rather do without." The train came to a complete stop at the 47th street station, I got up, got off and rode the escalator to street level. I lived about three blocks away, which normally took me about 15 minutes to walk home. But, this day, walking wasn't an option, I ran all the way home, and didn't stop until I reached my cousin's house. I ran up the stairs and banged on the door like the police with a warrant! "Cuz, cuz," I yelled! He snatched the door open with anger! "Man, what the f---k you knocking like that for!" he shouted. I pushed my way past him, and walked into the living room and took a seat. The house was a total wreck! Dirty dishes in the sink, the garbage was running over, spilling onto the floor. The living room table was littered with empty crack bags, beer cans and wine bottles. He used to be one of the biggest drug dealers in the hood, but, he had broken the game's number one rule; don't get high on your own supply. I had seen him go from riches to rags in a matter of months. The devil's love potion had him in it's grip, and he was in love, nothing else mattered but the glass pipe. It was really sad to see what crack had done to him. He had lost everything, including his sanity, but, he wouldn't stop. He got high from morning to night, seven days a week.

As I sat there looking around at the trash all over the apartment, I couldn't help but notice how unconcerned he was. It was like, he didn't have a care in the world, and his life could've been better. His situation didn't seem to bother him one iota. He was thinking about his next hit. He started crawling around the floor picking up everything white, hoping it was a piece of crack he had dropped, placing it on the broken mirror he had on the coffee table, burning it, praying it melted. I sat there watching him, wondering how it felt to be a hostage to such a condition. He crawled for hours, talking to himself, tasting tiny pieces of drywall, rice and paint chips, hoping to put together that one last hit. He was at his worst, and I found myself silently praying for him, asking God to relieve him of his misery. I opened my mouth to speak, but, the words froze themselves at the tip of my tongue, and in one quick motion, I reached in my pocket and handed him a 50 dollar bill. His eyes lit up like a spot light! He stood erect, cuffing the 50 dollar bill like it was going to save his life. Suddenly, for him, everything would be okay now.

Giving him the money wasn't probably the greatest thing I could've done for him, but, I couldn't bear watching him in that state of mind any longer. He needed to be rescued, if only for a short while.

He grabbed his keys and headed for the front door. Even though he had lost everything, he somehow managed to hold onto his burgundy 1976 ninety eight oldsmobile. It wasn't in mint condition, but, it would get you where you needed to go. It was the only thing crack hadn't took from him.

I sat there patiently while he went on the journey he loved most. About three blocks from where we lived, stood a 3 story red brick building at the corner of 53rd and princeton. The building was abandoned, except for the third floor apartment, it had been occupied by a man name Pettie. Pettie was a middle age man, a well known member of the Cobra Stones street gang that had controlled the streets of the low-end for years. He was six three, dark complexion, and his face was the look of stone. He had huge hands, and a strong deep voice that demanded attention. The apartment was his bread and butter. He sold 50 dollar bags of cocaine from the back door of the apartment 24 hours a day, seven days a week. His business was booming. Out of the hands of Pettie the devil's love potion moved through our neighborhood like a tsunami, destroying everything in it's path.

About 20 minutes had gone by when Cuz walked through the front door. He put his keys down on the kitchen table, and took a seat on the living room sofa in front of the broken mirror he used to prepare his misery. But, to him, it wasn't misery, it was just what he needed to medicate the pain he was feeling. His life was at rock bottom, and the crack was his only escape from reality.

I watched him open the small bag and pour out the powdery white substance on the broken mirror in front of him. The powder sparkled like tiny bits of diamonds, as he spread it out, chopping up the tiny chunks with a single edge razor blade. He then added a very small amount of baking soda to his chemical madness, and mixed it in with the powder. He concentrated, never giving his focus to anything else, he scooped it all up with a torn match book and put it in a glass tube. I Watched him closely, I was drawn in in amazement, anticipating what the outcome would be, wondering how he was gonna make this possible. He put two tablespoons of warm water in the glass tube, struck his cigarette lighter, and held the flame under the bottom of the tube. The mixture began to boil and bubble up and down until the powder turned into a gel like form, it fell to the bottom of the tube, and the preparation was done. He went to the kitchen sink, and held the tube under some cold water, and within seconds, the gel like substance hardened into one big rock.

You could see the joy of success in his dim lit eyes, he had prepared his escape from reality with perfect precision, and now, for the next 2 hours he would be somewhere where his present situation had no place. He would be in a secluded world of perfect bliss! No worries, no problems, just a temporary state of false happiness. The kind of happiness only man can create, and he had become a genius at creating his own.

I stared in awe, as Cuz dropped the finished product on the broken mirror. " It seemed so harmless," I thought to myself. How could something so small cause so much destruction? It was about the size of a small marble, but, it packed a powerful punch! He cut the rock up in tiny pebbles and crushed them with a spoon, transforming it back into powder form. He scooped up a considerable portion and put it on his glass pipe. He held it to his lips while he burned the powder with a torch he had made out of a broken clothes hanger with a ball of cotton wrapped around the end, that had been soaked in grain alcohol. He inhaled and the glass clouded up with thick white smoke that entered his system with vengeance. His eyes widened as the smoke took effect. He was on his way to that place he had come to know only when he was high. That place where he wished he could've never returned from. That place that erased everything unwanted in his mind. He blew out the smoke, and pain disguised itself as paradise, once again, he had sold his soul to satan.

I watched the thick white smoke escape his lips and engulf the room. I saw the calmness it gave him, and the look of peace that overwhelmed his presence. He was a new creature, that look of despair was no more, and he smiled. He put the pipe down and fell back onto the sofa, totally relaxed, he looked at me and said, "thank you cuz, thank you, I needed that."

CHAPTER 2

IT WAS ONE OF THOSE STICKY hot humid days in June. I had just left my cousin's apartment watching him get high. I sat on my front porch, thinking about Nedra and what I'd just experienced. Something inside of me needed that feeling Cuz felt. I had snorted cocaine before, but, I didn't remember enjoying it the way I saw Cuz enjoying it. I remembered being completely numb and paranoid. Not elated and happy like he seemed. If that one hit I saw him take could erase all the pain and misery I knew he was going through, I convinced myself, that what I was feeling would be nothing to eliminate. I stood up and reached into my pocket to count my money. I had recently gotten my student loan, and I still had about $1500 left after purchasing my DJ equipment. The curiosity in me was overwhelming, I had to try it. I had to know what he felt. I had to know what it was in that little white rock that brought him so much peace. Even though I knew his serenity seemed short lived, something in me still craved that feeling.

Filled with adrenaline, and extremely confused, I ran down my front steps, ready to test the water. Within seconds, I was at Cuz's front door once again, only this time the party would be on me. I guess the noise I made running up his steps, startled him. Before I could knock, he opened the door, "what's up cuz," he said, looking at me strangely. I walked pass him, and told him to close the door. I felt this sudden rush of guilt pass over me, as if I'd done something horribly wrong. It was like a warning, trying desperately to redirect me. But, it was too late, my mind was made up, and I had made the decision final. I sat down on the living room couch, and stared at the remaining crack Cuz had left on the broken mirror. Cuz looked at me as though he knew what I was thinking. Before I could utter a word, he scooped up a small portion of the broken rock and put it on the pipe. He held it to my lips, as he lit the torch, putting the flame to the pipe, he said, "pull, pull, and keep pulling." I followed instructions until I was almost out of breath. "Stop pulling and hold the smoke," he said. I held it as long as I could, and out of my mouth, came a thick white cloud, the drug took effect immediately! A warm inviting sensation filled my body from my head to my feet, it felt better than the moment before climaxing! My hands tingled, and my penis stood erect, it felt as if I was ejaculating repeadly. The intensity of the hit lasted about 10 minutes, and it was gone just as quickly as it had came. I looked at Cuz and said, "DAMN," it was the only word I could muster up. He knew I had made the worst decision of my life, and he had done nothing to stop me.

That sense of guilt washed over me even stronger this time as the high started to wear off. As I began to sober up, I felt this unbearable mood of depression, I hadn't anticipated this. I had to have more, I needed to find that feeling again and never let it go.

In the beginning, I wasn't totally addicted. I still kept my life in order somewhat. It wasn't until the end of the summer when I started getting high every chance I got. At first it was just a weekend thing, and as time went on it progressed. But, I still couldn't see it was bringing me down a piece at a time. As long as I looked good, stayed in school and kept money in my pocket, I was alright.

I was blinded by the reality of what drugs could do. Even after I saw what it done to Cuz, I still believed I was in control.

I never considered that maybe this life was destined to be. Growing up in a dysfunctional home, and enduring my Father's alcoholism, was enough to misdirect anyone's sanity. I promised myself I would never let anyone or anything control me like that, and now I had indulged in something much worse than alcohol.

I sat on the couch, staring at the broken mirror, secretly wishing we had more crack. I thought long and hard about what I was doing, but, the grip of the devil's love potion had already sunk it's claws in me from the very first hit.

I lifted my eyes from that dark stare the drugs had me captivated by, and glanced around the room at the filth and garbage Cuz had allowed to accumulate in his little secluded dungeon. A memory of how he used to be, flashed in front of me so vividly, it seemed like we had gone back in the past, when the drugs wasn't a part of his life. A time when he had it all together, for that brief moment, we were there again and all was well. But, no matter how I day dreamed, the reality of the circumstances were ever so real! He was strung out, and the pipe was his only friend.

CHAPTER 3

I WENT THE SCHOOL THE NEXT day trying hard to forget the night before. I couldn't get the images out of my mind. I kept visualizing the thick white smoke traveling through the pipe like a long stream of fluffy cotton. I sat there in class, my body present, but, my mind in some distant place, surrounded by that feeling. It was no use, I couldn't focus and I couldn't wait for class to end.

Somehow, I had to get a grip on myself. It was my first time, there was no way I could be addicted this quick. Cuz wasn't the first person I'd seen drugs destroy, and none of them had went to rags over night, it was a process to this madness. I mean, even my father didn't become an alcoholic overnight, he was a functioning alcoholic for years before he lost control.

After class, I sat in the student lounge twirling my thumbs in deep thought. I hadn't fully committed to this new lifestyle, and my inner man was fighting with vengeance against the darkness that dwelled in me. It made me wonder if this entity had been awaiting its chance to surface all along.

Or was I just in the wrong place at the wrong time. The different theories scattered themselves in my mind, and I was still without a solution or reasonable answer to the choices I had made. Excuses wouldn't help, I'd seen enough to know I should've never tried it. But, what now? Do I continue to flirt with satan, or do I stand against him? My mind went blank, I couldn't seem to find common ground, or even enough faith to fight him. I got up and left the student lounge, headed for the el-train with one thing on my mind, that feeling. I had to have it one more time.

The anticipation of that next hit had my stomach doing flips, it was crazy! It would be my second time doing it, and already, something inside me was drawing me to it, the want became physical, I could feel it.

I sat suspiciously on the train, patting my pockets, making sure my money was still there. My mind and body captured by a high I hadn't got yet. It was as if the thought of it teased me just enough to keep me from changing my mind; and suddenly, the train came to a complete stop at the 47th street station.

Something inside of me wanted to remain sitting, but, it wasn't strong enough. It seemed to be calling me with a secret voice that only I could hear, a voice destined for my ears only, a voice that not even God could hear, or at least that's what I thought.

I got off the train walking frantically toward my house, hoping Cuz would be home. I had known Pettie well enough to get the product myself, but, I didn't want nobody to know my business. The closer I got to that dungeon Cuz lived in, the more my stomach flipped. I wondered had he gotten past that stage, was his stomach flipping like mine? My soul kept questioning my conscious, but, there were no answers. Over and over I could feel the effect of the drug, while I mentally entertained the thought of how much to buy.

Within the next five minutes, I was there a second time, standing at the entrance of defeat. The door was slightly ajar. I peaked in calling his name, "Cuz, you in here," I whispered as I walked in, closing the door behind me. The apartment was still a mess, and the stench was almost breathtaking. A strong odor of urine and feces escaped from the bathroom. I moved quickly past the toxic area and into the living room as if the smell would be left behind me. Frantically, I opened every window, desperately hoping some fresh air would rush in. Stepping over empty beer cans and wine bottles, I found Cuz on the floor in a death like sleep. His hair was matted, and his clothes were dirty. I looked down at his stomach to see if he was breathing, and he was. A sudden sigh of relief fell over me, I thought to myself, "thank God he's not dead." I shook him violently, trying to bring him out his comatose like state. Again and again I tried, until his eyes opened. "Cuz, you alright?" I asked. His eyes were bloodshot red, and his skin looked dark and burnt. The results of a week with no sleep and nourishment, displayed itself throughout his entire countenance, he was dehydrated and exhausted. He had been on a binge and his body had shut down. The effects of his addiction were extremely noticeable, and no matter what he did, there was no disguising it.

For a brief moment, the reason I was there eluded me, and pity took over. Suddenly, I wanted to help him instead of enabling him. But, I needed him to score for me, I wanted to get high. I paid no attention to what drugs had done to him, in my mind he was weak, yet, I still felt sorry for him. "Maybe a hit is what he needed," I thought to myself as I helped him get up off the floor, and take a seat on the worn out and stained sofa. The black leather three piece living room set was once a attraction to the small one bedroom apartment, but now it was worn and mutilated from weeks and months of neglect. He got up and walked into the kitchen, sorting through the dirty dishes, he found a small pot and filled it with warm water. "I need coffee," he said, "strong black coffee, it's the only thing that will wake me up." I sat patiently until he had prepared the steaming hot cup of mud, and joined me in front of the broken mirror.

It was no secret, Cuz knew why I was there. He knew I was back for that feeling I got from that first hit. He knew all too well what it was like. It was that same feeling he had been chasing from the very first time he tried the drug. I reached in my pocket and pulled out a hundred dollar bill, and passed to him. "Here ya go Cuz, go get us two," I said, with a slight tremble in my voice. My hands were sweating, my stomach was boiling, and my pulse was racing in anticipation of the consumption of the devil's love potion. It was real now as I visualized the effect of the thick smoke that would soon occupy his pipe.

He seemed to have no strength, the coffee had awaken him, but, he still lacked the energy to make the journey needed to score for us. He sat there another twenty minutes, sipping on the piping hot coffee until he was able to move.

Suddenly, it wasn't the high that fascinated me, it was the destruction it caused that instantly scared the shit outta me! "Is this how I'm gonna end up, strung out, nasty, and completely insane!" I questioned myself in a one on one conversation with my conscious. I was ignoring God, he was speaking to me and I knew it, but, the devil's voice spoke even louder.

My lack of faith had finally gotten the best of me, I felt almost just as weak as Cuz did. I watched him walk out the door and down the steps to his car. As I sat there alone, waiting for Cuz to return, my life flashed in front of me. I got a glimpse of my own destruction, I could see myself in the same situations, and the same circumstances as Cuz. Somehow, someway, I had to stay in control. I couldn't let that feeling destroy me! "I can handle it," I told myself. And before I knew it, Cuz walked in with the my misery wrapped in a small colorful bag.

CHAPTER 4

I REMEMBER WAKING UP THE NEXT morning not knowing when or how I got home. I only lived two houses away from Cuz, but still, I couldn't remember how I got there. I was still dressed in the clothes I had on the night before, and I hadn't even taken off my gym shoes. I had a splitting headache, and my hands and fingernails were dirty as if I'd been planting flowers in a garden all day.

I sat up on the side of my bed, trying to recall the events that had taken place the previous night, and then it hit me. Suddenly, my mind painted a vivid picture of me at the dungeon with Cuz. We had been smoking crack all night!

I could hear my mom in the bathroom getting ready for work. I couldn't let her see me, I looked a mess! I closed my bedroom door, and pretended to be asleep. While I laid there waiting for my mother to leave for work, I thought about Cuz and what drugs had done to his life, I had seen it with my own eyes. But, he wasn't the only one. Crack had began its destruction in a lot of families in my neighborhood. Almost everyone I knew was using something; crack, heroin, cocaine, marijuana, some was using them all. Although, some of them kept their business behind closed doors, some of them didn't care who knew.

Finally, I heard the front door close, and mom was off to work. My first class started at 11 a.m. but, I hadn't gotten enough rest, and I looked like a storm had ripped through me! I stood in front of the bathroom mirror, gazing at the image looking back at me. My eyes were dim and red, lacking that glow they normally had. My face wasn't my face, it's countenance had changed overnight. I wasn't sure if anyone else would notice, but, I did. I splashed cold water on my face, hoping to remove this unwanted appearance. The effect of the drugs took over, I couldn't mask the evidence. "Was this the beginning of my destruction," I thought to myself. I splashed more cold water on my face, trying to conceal the obvious, but, again the aftermath of the drugs took over. There was no use, it was written all over my face. I was a hostage, captivated by the devil's love potion, and there was no negotiating my freedom.

The guilt of what I'd done was overwhelming, I was terrified! That morning I sat on the living room couch thinking about how I could continue this madness without losing control. I had ruled out the option of never doing it again, I had fallen in love the very first hit. The thought of becoming like Cuz scared the shit outta me, but, I was still willing to take the chance, thinking things would be different.

I decided not to go to class that morning, so, I got dressed, and headed for Cuz's house. I knew he would be there, probably getting high or drinking his morning cup of coffee. He was never sober, mainly because he ran his apartment with open doors to whoever had some crack to share with him. People came and went all day everyday, bringing those small bags of misery with them that helped them escape the nightmares they couldn't seem to wake up from. His apartment was like a graveyard for restless souls who couldn't find permanent peace. They moved around like zombies, eyes wide open, staring into space, seemingly praying for that next hit, or to be rescued from their madness.

As I made my way up the stairs to Cuz's front door, it seem unusually quiet, it wasn't the same. Usually, this early in the morning the door would be wide open, and Cuz would be up, drinking his routine cup of coffee. I stood at the door silently, listening for any activity inside the dungeon, there was none. I hesitated before I knocked, peeking in the window, I could see Cuz lying on the living room floor appearing to be asleep. I had found him like this before, but, this time it felt different, something was wrong. I tapped on the window with a coin, hoping to wake him, but, he wasn't moving. I banged on the door with my fist tightly balled up, "Cuz, Cuz," I yelled! Still, no answer. I peeked back through the window to see if he had gotten up, but, he was still in the same position, face down in the middle of the floor.

My hair stood up on my arms at the thought of him being dead. "Should I kick the door open, should I call the police?" A thousand thoughts rushed me, while I stood there trying to decide what to do. Had he overdosed, or was he just in a deep sleep? Either way, I had to get in. I took two steps back, and with my right foot, I kicked the door open with force! Surprisingly, the noise didn't appear to alarm the neighbors, nobody came to see what had happened.

I could see him more clearly now. I was in the dungeon, standing in the middle of the kitchen floor, looking at his lifeless body stretched out on the floor like a worn out carpet, he looked a mess. "Maybe he had taken his last hit, maybe his heart had all it could take," I thought to myself. I walked closer to him to get a better look, he seemed stiff. His face had a stressful expression on it, and it didn't look like he was breathing. "Damn Cuz, what the f--k did you do?' I said aloud, hoping that maybe the sound of my voice would wake him. Just as I reached down to shake him, he rolled over and sat straight up, eyes wide open. My first thought said, "run," but my legs wouldn't move. 'Damn Cuz," I yelled, "you scared the shit outta me.! My pulse was escalated, and my heart was beating off the meter.

A part of me was glad that he wasn't dead, but, a part of me wanted to get high. I helped him up off the floor and sat him on the old dingy leather sofa. His countenance displayed years of pain, suffering and abuse. He looked at me, struggling to put together an excuse for the way I'd found him. As much as he wanted to, he had nothing or nobody to blame for what he'd done to his own life. He had knew the consequences, and yet, he found himself at the bottom of the barrow with no will to reach the top. His body had shut down and miraculously revived itself again. He had only God to thank for another chance at life. He sat there with pride, as though God owed him one, and he had been compensated. He leaned forward, and looked me directly in my eye, the words rolled hopelessly off his lips, "let's get high."

CHAPTER 5

THAT MORNING SHOULD'VE BEEN A WAKE up call for me. Seeing Cuz in that condition scared me motionlessness, I couldn't move! The reality of the horrors of addition were revealing themselves to me one at a time. I had seen it many times before, but, then I was on the outside looking in, now I was caught smack in the middle.

For the first time, the birds were chirping when I walked through my front door. The sun was out, shining bright and hot over my neighborhood. It was a few minutes passed eight, and mom had already left for work. This was the second day in a row I'd been out all night getting high. Cuz was the neighborhood chemist, and he made it almost impossible to excuse yourself from the broken mirror. He had a unique way of cooking the cocaine and bringing it back to its purest form, making it more potent when we smoked it. Everybody knew of his skills, he was the cook for the majority of the addicts from 51st and princeton to 41st and princeton. He had so much traffic, he couldn't get clean if he wanted to, he never got the chance, people were coming and going all day and all night.

This was the second day for me, and I was totally exhausted. Once again I had managed to escape confrontation with my mom. I walked in my room, and flopped across the bed. My hands and fingernails were even dirtier than the first time I stayed out all night. But, this time, my appearance was even more disgusting than the last. My clothes were dirty and smelly from all the sweating I'd been doing in the dungeon Cuz lived in. He didn't have a air condition, and the fan he had only circulated the hot air.

I had to get myself together, I knew I wouldn't be going to school this day either. I kept telling myself, "I'll make up the classes," but, the truth was, I never did.

Finally, I got up and went to the bathroom to attend to my hygiene. My father was on his way back from Mississippi picking up my Grandmother. There was no way I was gonna let them see me this way.

I rambled through my closet frantically looking for something wear. My father had phoned and said, they were only an hour away. That didn't leave me much time to do everything I needed to do, so, I decided to shave first.

I stood in the bathroom mirror looking at someone else's face. Once again, the effects of the drugs had did a number on me, disfiguring my appearance. Suddenly, I realized, shaving and cutting my hair wasn't gonna hide this stranger I was looking at. I needed to do the best I could, and get the hell outta the house before they got there. I finished what I could, cleaned up my mess, and went back over Cuz's house.

I was surprised to see Cuz up, and moving around. He was cleaning up the dungeon, I was shocked! For a brief moment, I didn't see him as the lost soul he was. He had cleaned himself up, and put on some clean clothes. He couldn't hide the battle scars from all the years of drug abuse, but, at least it was a start. Even if it didn't last long, it showed me there was still hope. Just to see him taking some interest in himself was enough for me.

I watched Cuz clean the dungeon like a seasoned maid, every beer can, wine bottle, and crack bag were gone. For the first time in a long time, I didn't smell the stench of urine and feces in the air. "Damn Cuz, it's looking good and smelling good in here."

I sat on the living room sofa while Cuz finished up the final touches of his cleaning task. He had gotten the apartment in order, and put on some water to prepare his morning cup of coffee.

I felt guilty sitting there thinking about getting high. The change I'd seen in Cuz was great, but, it confused me. Was he done with the life? Had he taken his last hit? I looked at the coffee table, and noticed the broken mirror missing. Razor blades, pipes, baking soda, and anything else needed to prepare the drug, was gone, Cuz had cleaned house!

He put away his cleaning supplies, and took a seat on the worn out leather recliner he found in the alley behind his house. God only know's what it was that attracted him to it; maybe it was the color, it matched the sofa, but, that was the only feature I saw. I had saw the worn out chair many times when I took out the garbage. Stray dogs and cats had sleep on it most of the summer. But, that didn't matter to Cuz, to him it was his own personal chair, and he didn't let nobody sit in it but himself.

Getting rid of all the trash seem to give the place a different feel. But, no matter how I tried to shun the negative thoughts, it was still the dungeon to me, and I knew the cleanliness wouldn't last long. Cuz was ready to break out the broken mirror, and so was I, I could see it in his eyes. He was ready to reward himself, and I had the money to kick things off!

We drunk a six pack of beer, and smoked a joint to get the party started. Unlike before, the beer and weed had started to set me up for the main course. The urge for crack was getting stronger the more intoxicated I became. "That's strange,' I thought to myself. Cuz stared at me, it was like he knew the cravings were increasing. He knew from his own experience, I was waving my feet in some deep water, and again he said nothing to discourage me.

As much as I wanted to believe he cared if drugs ruined my life, I knew the only thing that mattered to him was that next hit, my life was worth nothing compared to his pipe. We both sat there quietly, trying to read each other's mind, while we finished up the last of the joint. After all the beer and weed was gone, we both knew what came next.

Cuz got up and walked into the kitchen, he returned with the broken mirror in his hand. He sat it down cautiously on the coffee table next to a small leather traveling bag. The bag had been sitting there the whole time, and I never noticed it. Mentally captivated by the anticipation of getting high, I had overlooked the leather bag.

I glanced down at the broken mirror, wondering how many people had poured their problems out on its surface. The more I stared at it, the more I could visualize the pain it reflected. Jobs, homes, cars, bank accounts, peace of mind, and sanity all rolled up in one, had been dropped in a glass tube, cooked up, placed on a pipe and turned into a puff of smoke. The mirror was a reflection of misery, patiently waiting for our donation.

Cuz unzipped the leather bag, and exposed its contents. Razor blades, glass tubes, baking soda, and pipes filled the interior. Everything we needed to add fuel to the fire was there, except the main ingredient, cocaine.

CHAPTER 6

I COULD SEE MY FATHER'S CAR from Cuz's kitchen window. He had arrived over an hour ago with my grandma. I couldn't risk the chance of my father seeing me, I wasn't exactly looking like myself. I had done the best I could with the little time I had to get myself together, but, the evidence was still there. I wasn't sure my father would figure things out, so, I stayed outta sight while Cuz went to cop for us.

I sat on the sofa twirling my thumbs, looking out the window. Cuz had only been gone a few minutes when I decided to speed up the process. All the tools we needed were right in front of me. I poured everything outta the bag on the broken mirror. I had watched Cuz many times set up the works, I knew what to do. But, I hadn't learned to cook yet, and I wasn't sure if I wanted to learn, but, the whole chemical process was fascinating to watch.

Finally, Cuz walked in with the product. "Damn cuz,' he said with a smile in his tone. "You got everything set up, I see you been paying attention.' Cuz open the small package and poured the powder on the mirror. I passed him a razor blade, and he began breaking down the tiny pebbles.

Within seconds, he had it all in the glass tube, and the chef went to work!

I watched him closely this time, as he prepared another dose of misery for us. He cooked the product like he was preparing dinner for the president, one step at a time, with precision. He blew out the flame, and added the cold water for the finishing touch. The jelly substance hardened into one marble sized rock, and it was done.

He dropped it on the mirror. It was solid and white, hiding its real intentions. Cuz chopped it up with a razor blade, and put a piece on his pipe. It was his first hit of the day, and it took effect before he could put the pipe down. I looked at him standing in the middle of the floor, eyes bucked with a ghostly stare. He was right where he what to be, trapped in that feeling.

I watched the smoke as it continued to escape from his lips. He fell back on his leather recliner, and let out a loud sigh, a sudden look of peace swam over his face. Whatever had been worrying him, was over now, and all was calm for the moment.

I briefly hesitated before I picked up the pipe. I was still watching the effect it had on Cuz. He was still sitting there with that ghostly look in his eyes, looking like he wanted to speak, but couldn't. I wanted that feeling too, but, Cuz was scaring the shit outta me! "Dude, you alright," I asked, my voice trembling. He opened his mouth to answer me, but, he couldn't seem to form the words, the crack had him stuck!

He sat there the next thirty minutes, staring into space, not blinking. 'Damn," I whispered to myself, "he high as hell, I don't know if I should try this batch." A part of me wanted to get up and walk out, but, the curiosity of what he was feeling took over me, and I picked up the pipe.

The first hit was so potent, I sat the pipe down, and joined Cuz in a staring contest. We both sat there, looking at the ceiling like we could see straight through it! I was there, where ever there was. I kept feeling like I wanted to move, but, I couldn't. I wanted to speak, but, I couldn't. I sat on the sofa, froze, clenching my teeth so tight, you couldn't pry them apart with a crowbar. My hearing intensified, I could hear conversations outside, but, couldn't make out what they were saying. I focused on the front door, waiting for the police to kick it in. The paranoia had gotten the best of me, the crack had me scared shittless!

I barricaded myself in Cuz's apartment the rest of the evening. The high had never lasted that long, and had never been that potent. The sun had gone down, and hours had past by like minutes. But, Cuz hadn't stop smoking. He was taking hit after hit, trying to get that first one back.

Suddenly, the paranoia left just as quickly as it had came, and the calmness set in. Boy, was I ever so glad that was over. I thought I was about to lose my mind.

I didn't understand how it was so strong. I watched him cook it, and he hadn't done anything different. It made me wonder if he had put something in it before he came back. But, why would he do that? The questions flooded my thoughts in vain, I didn't have an answer to any of them.

I rolled me another joint to help me mask the effect of the powerful rock. Staring at the broken mirror, the thought of taking one more hit invaded me. "One more," I told myself, "just one more, and I'm going home."

Cuz was in his own world, crawling around the floor, picking up everything white. He didn't even notice when I picked up the pipe and packed it with the biggest hit I had ever taken. I lit the torch, and started pulling. Immediately, the glass filled up with a thick white cloud that entered my system with vengeance! The high was intense, but, it brought pain with it this time. A pain that hit the center of my chest with force, causing me to drop the pipe, and the lit torch. For a split second, the room went dark, I couldn't see a thing! I was scared, and gasping for air. The chest pains got more and more intense, and then my sight returned as I fell backwards, hitting the floor like a solid piece wood!

Cuz snapped out of it, and regained his senses. "Cuz, cuz," he kept yelling! I could hear him, but, it sounded like his voice was in some distant place. I laid flat on my back, trying to speak, but, I couldn't. My mind tried hard to communicate with my body, but, there was no use. I was having a heart attack, and death was staring me dead in the face!

I didn't know how long I'd been laying there, but, it seemed like forever. I could feel a tear glide down my face as the pain got worse. Cuz leaned over me with a strange look in his eyes. He looked confused, like he didn;t know if he should get help or not. He grabbed my right arm, and dragged me across the floor like a wet mop. Suddenly, it occurred to me he wasn't trying to help me, he was trying to get me out of his house.

He opened the door, drug my pain stricken body out onto his back porch and slammed it shut I tried to roll myself over and stand up, but, the pain was to severe. Something was pulling my chest apart from the inside out. The stabbing pains came repeatedly, one after the other. I kept telling myself, "If I'm gonna die, I'm not gonna die on no damn porch!

Although the pain was unbearable, I managed to stand on my feet. Holding the banister, I walked down the steps, one at a time until I reached the bottom. I lifted my head, trying to focus, but , my vision was blurry. I began to call on God, as I slowly moved down the long gangway. I was almost there, "just a little bit further," I told God. "Just a little bit further, and I'll be home."

I had convinced myself, If I could make it home, everything would be alright. I could see my front porch, as I cleared the entrance to Cuz's gangway, I was almost there," just a few feet more, please God," I begged. All of a sudden, I felt a push in the center of my back that made me stumble forward. It was as if something was helping me shorten my journey. I turned to look, and there was no one there.

I kneeled down at bottom step on my porch, and crawled to my front door. The pain had subsided a little, and I was able to get my key in the door. God was aiding me, but, I didn't know it then. How selfish of me to think I was doing it all on my own. I just needed to get to my room and relax, and maybe the pain would go away.

Miraculously, I made it inside to find everyone asleep. My father was on the dining room couch in a deep sleep, probably worn out from the long drive back from Mississippi. I tried hard not to make any noise, as the pain rolled back up in the center of my chest, challenging my life again. Despite the agony I was feeling, I manage to creep past my father, and make it to my room. I got in bed, to weak and in to much pain to be concerned with getting undressed, I tried to lay still, hoping it would somehow make a difference. And then it happened again! The pain hit me in the same spot, but, this time it came twice as strong as the first. I tried to scream for help, but, my wind left my body, and I couldn't breath. I banged on the my bedroom wall, hoping to wake someone up, but, no one heard me. I rolled myself outta the bed, and hit the floor like a ton of bricks! I crawled to the kitchen floor, and the light came on. For a brief second, everything seemed unusually bright, and then just as quick, everything went dark. For that very short moment, I had lost life.

Strangely, I remember wondering if I was going to heaven or hell. I could hear my mother screaming, "don't let my baby die!" The pain was gone, and my body felt weird. I could see my father sitting on top of me pounding on my chest, but, I couldn't feel the blows. I was somewhere else, but, still in my house. I was in two different places at the same time. I was standing behind my father looking down at me. He was trying frantically to bring me back. He kept pounding, but, still I felt nothing. The sound of each blow, played an alarming rhythm of bass that echoed throughout my conscious. "Wake up boy, wake your ass up," he shouted! His voice seem to be fading each time he screamed the words. Again, a tear glided down the side of my face, disappearing somewhere behind my ear. The silhouette image of me repositioned itself behind my mother, and patted her softly on the shoulder, attempting to comfort her. And then I heard it! The sound of daddy's voice got closer and closer, I saw the ghostly image of me lift itself from the floor, and dematerialized into air, it fell directly on top of me, jolting me out of the lifeless state. My body twitched violently, returning from a visit with death! "He's alive, he's alive," my mother shouted! "Thank you Jesus, my baby is alive."

I laid in the hospital for the first five days of a two week stay, thinking about the bad decisions I made that put me there. It was my first brush with death, and it scared the shit outta me! The vivid images of the heart attack kept flashing in front of me. Cuz had left me for dead, and put me on his porch like used garbage. I remembered everything, from beginning to end, and I vowed to kick his ass as soon as I got well.

The heart attack was a rude awakening for me, but, the feeling of the high was still present. A part of me was trying to delete the thought of it, but, a part of was still craving more, and little did i know, there was plenty of pain left.

CHAPTER 7

MY SECRET WAS OUT NOW. THE heart attack I had woke everybody up! My mother was heartbroken, and angry at the same. My sister was severely disappointed at even the thought of me using drugs of any kind. She tried hard to set a path of success for me, monitoring my education, and helping me academically when I needed it. I watched her all my life, accomplishing one goal after another, completing every task put in front of her with extreme commitment. She had lead by example my entire life, and I followed her to the best of my ability, until now. I felt like a little kid, needing to be taught right from wrong. Drugs were a no no in my family, and I knew it.

A week later I was discharged from the hospital with strict instructions to stay away from drugs. I had no intentions of ever trying crack again, but, I knew I would never stop smoking weed. I had tried it for the first time at twelve years old, and loved it! It only had three stages; funny, hungry, and sleepy, and neither stage had ever harmed me in any way. Seeing what alcohol had done to my father, completely discouraged me from drinking. I had saw him plenty times on his knees in the bathroom, praying to the porcelain god, sick from the consumption of hard liquor, begging God to sober him up, and he would never do it again.

I sat on the front porch that afternoon, replaying that scary night in my head. The thought of what happened sent chills down my spine considering how close I came to permanently checking out. The tiny slides lined themselves up frame by frame like a movie, detailing everything that happened. I had kissed death directly in the mouth, and had lived to tell my story.

Suddenly, I had a new appreciation for life. But, in the back of mind, I knew the opportunity to get high would present itself again, I only hoped I would be strong enough to resist it.

The news spread like running water through the hood. For some, it was just what they wanted to see. Jealousy was like a poison, corrupting the hearts of people I had known for years, hiding behind smiles, and fake laughter, pretending to be a friend. My mother had preached to me many times about trusting people to easily, letting them in without earning the right to there.

Nevertheless, I was thick headed and disobedient, thinking I had all the answers. I was a big boy now. I had survived a heart attack, and if that didn't kill me, nothing could! I be damned, if I was gonna let a small white pebble take me out!

An hour had swiftly passed by, when my eyes refocused on my sister parking in front my house. She got out of the car with an unfamiliar look on her face, she was pissed! I had never seen her mad before, and the way she was approaching, made me nervous. I tried to prep what to say, but, I was lost for words, she had caught me totally off guard.

She stopped at the bottom of the stairs, and looked up at me with disappointment in her eyes. She was hurt! Guilt washed over me, as I took a deep breath, and prepared myself for the verbal abuse. "Have you lost your mind," she shouted! "Cocaine Derrick, are you crazy!" I had no defense, my mouth flung open, but, nothing came out. "I've already made arrangements for you to get help. It's a six month inpatient treatment facility, and its not open for discussion."

"Treatment facility," I thought to myself, "that's for addicts." I wasn't homeless, living on the street eatin outta garbage cans, stealing and robbing for money to get high. "I had it all under control, I just put a little much on the pipe," I told myself.

After sitting attentively, and letting my sister vent, I agreed to the six month program, still not believing I needed help. Why was she coming down on me so hard, I Wasn't like Cuz. I'd only done it a few times, and my life was still pretty much in order. I had money in my pocket, I looked good, I was still in school, and I got high when I wanted to, I wasn't addicted.

My sister walked away from the porch, getting in her car, she look back at me and said, " I'll be back in a hour to pick you up, be ready." "Be ready," she said. Those two words planted themselves in my conscious with a profound meaning other than what she intended it to mean.

I sat on my bed, trying to imagine what treatment would be like. Living with people, admitting they were strung out on drugs like it was something to be proud of. To me, it wasn't that bad, I was having fun. I wasn't strung out, and I damn sho wasn't about to admit I was an addict. Even I knew words were powerful, and if I admitted defeat, I Would eventually start believing it.

I packed my clothes and sat patiently waiting for my sister to return. Six months in this place was sure to teach me something, but, what. I tried to keep an open mind about the whole thing, I just couldn't see myself that weak. I was always taught that drugs were for weak people, people who couldn't deal with life on life's terms. People who needed something to help them escape reality.

The more I thought about it, the more I considered the fact, that I might need help, but, just didn't understand the severity of my denial.

The doorbell rang, jolting me outta my deep thoughts. I knew it was my sister, so I grab my suitcase, trying to look in compliance with the decision she'd made to get me help. I always valued my sister's opinion about anything concerning my life, and I always benefitted from listening from her advice.

The ride to the facility was quiet, neither of us said a word the whole trip. The silence was killing me. I had no idea what to expect from this place where I would be surrounded by real drug addicts. I had heard about these programs where people talked about their struggles, how they lost everything, and in most cases ended up homeless, eating outta garbage cans, panhandling and stealing to support their habits. I had yet to experience these horrors, and prayed, I never would, and hopefully this place would prevent it.

Finally, we arrived at the location. The facility had once been a dorm for college students, but, had recently been renovated, and turned into a rehabilitation center for substance abuse. I sat in the car, staring at the building, ashamed at the reason I was there. My sister got outta the car with a big smile on her face. "Wow, this is a nice place," she said. "Look at the scenery, everything looks so well kept." I couldn't agree with her more. The landscaping was beautiful! The grass was a glowing bright green, neatly groomed. The building was two stories high, professionally designed with huge glass windows overlooking the rest of the campus. It was a paradise for addicts. I had no idea it would be so inviting. "Get outta the car boy, come on," my sister shouted, waking me from my daydream.

As we walked up the steps to the huge glass doors, I turned to look at the free world as though it would be my last time seeing it. I felt like I was turning myself in to serve time for some criminal act I'd committed. I had never been confined in my life, and suddenly, I wasn't sure if I needed to be there.

I sat in the office with my sister, pretending to listen to the intake counselor while she explained the rules and regulations of the program, and repeatedly asking me to sign form after form. The facility was equipped with three separate programs; one for children under twelve, another for teenagers, and the other for adults. I had no idea a child could be an addict, and yet, this facility offered treatment, and housed kids.

The meeting with the counselor lasted about an hour. I walked my sister to her car, and went back inside. Immediately, the intake counselor showed me to my room. It was a considerable size room with four twin beds. Each bed had it's own nightstand and lamp. The whole scene was depressing, but, I knew I had to stick it out. Living in a room for six months with real hardcore drug addicts wasn't exactly how I pictured it, I thought I would have my own room.

I unpacked my suitcase, and put away my clothes. The counselor had given me a schedule, and I knew a meeting was about to start. I closed my bedroom door, and joined a crowd of teenagers headed down the hallway to where the meeting was held.

It was a huge open space, with tan carpet, and chairs neatly arranged in a circle. Four staff members sat at the front of the room behind a long brown table. I looked around the room as I took my seat. The walls were covered with posters, and written on them were encouraging statements, such as, "let go and let God, one day at a time, just for today, the serenity prayer, the twelve steps, and the twelve traditions of narcotics anonymous. Framed photographs were placed neatly on the wall, representing addicts who had completed the program successfully. "Damn," I thought to myself, "they take this whole addition thing serious."

The room was full, as the addicts got up one by one, admitting they were addicts, and their lives had become unmanageable. They shared stories of unbelievable horror! I sat there trembling inside, a lot of them were only kids, 15, 16, and 17 years old.

The meeting lasted about forty five minutes, and we closed with the serenity prayer; "God grant me the serenity to accept the things I cannot change, the courage to change the things I can, and the wisdom to know the difference." I had never heard a prayer so simple, short, and to the point.

The prayer was like a lifeline to them, they recited it with confidence.

The staff gave us a 15 minute break before the next group started. Some went outside to have a cigarette, while others went back to their rooms for whatever reason. I remained in my seat, thinking about the prayer, and trying to gather it's meaning. The words had planted themselves in my conscious, and I found myself reciting them over and over in my head.

I still wasn't sure if I needed to be there, but, that prayer, it was something about that prayer that captivated me, and then it hit me! I had been trying to change things I had no control over my whole life. Trying to make my mother leave my father because of the abuse. Trying to stop my father from drinking. I had endured a lot as a child, but, nothing had made my previous trials and tribulations more clear to me than that prayer.

After the short break, we all returned to the meeting room. I found myself standing, with my hand raised high. I wasn't sure I was an addict, but, I knew I had things buried in me, and it had to come out.

"Was it true, had my life become unmanageable?" The words rolled of my tongue like a movie script. The more I spoke, the more the pain found its way to the surface, bringing with it years of emotional, and mental abuse. I stood there for almost thirty minutes sharing my search for love in all the wrong places. The truth in me demanded its freedom, and I delivered it with conviction. The Addicts in the circle moved to the edge of their seats, each looking at me as though I had been their in the midst of some of their failures and defeats.. It was the first time in my life I had ever let anyone in on the hate I had bottled up in me for my father, or the betrayal I experienced over and over from my mother. I had found common ground, and it felt good to speak with rigorous honesty.

I sat down, no longer confused about how who I was or why I was there. I had issues that haunted me long before drugs were a part of my life. I was an adult child of an alcoholic father, and codependent mother who had inserted all their problems in me.

PART 2

CHAPTER 1

I COMPLETED THE SIX MONTH PROGRAM with honors. I walked out the front door with all the tools I needed to maintain sobriety. I memorized all of the little quotes of recovery, but, my favorite one was the philosophy……………..

"GOD, HELP US STAY CLEAN AND SOBER FOR TODAY! WE HAVE COME TOGETHER BECAUSE THERE IS NO EASY WAY. BECAUSE WE SEARCH STEP BY STEP FOR AWAY AND A LANGUAGE. A WAY TO SEE OURSELVES MORE CLEARLY, AND A LANGUAGE BY WHICH TO GIVE AND RECEIVE THE LOVE THAT IS SOMEWHERE HIDDEN IN EACH OF US.

THERE ARE EVERYWHERE, BLIND STREETS AND DEAD END ALLEYS, BUT TOGETHER WE CAN BUILD OPEN ROADS, OUR BAD CHOICES DO NOT ACCOUNT FOR FAILURES, ONLY MISTAKES. THE ONLY MISTAKES THAT ACCOUNT PERMANENTLY ARE NOT SO MUCH THE ERRORS THEMSELVES, WHICH ARE INEVITABLE, AS A WILLINGNESS TO BE DEFEATED BY THEM.

THE MOST PITIFUL THING IS, A PERSON WHO THINKS HE HAS NOTHING MORE TO LEARN; HE IS DEAD! FOR ALL THOSE PERSONS EXEMPT FROM GUILT AND DISHONESTY, SOMETIMES WE LOVE OUR GUILT AND DISHONESTY.

THIS HOUSE IS ONLY A BRIEF SHELTER ALONG THE WAY, MY BROTHERS AND SISTERS CAN ONLY EXTEND A HAND.

WHAT I AM, I CHOSE TO BE, AND BECAUSE I CHOOSE, I'M RESPONSIBLE. THERE IS ONLY ONE KIND OF MAGIC, AND THAT'S DOIN IT, SO LET'S DO IT!

Despite what I'd learned, the program hadn't done much for my denial, I still didn't believe I was an addict. I just knew I was messed up, but, I told myself drugs had nothing to do with it. I blamed everything on my parents, they were the reason for misdirections in life! But, the philosophy said, "if I choose, I'm responsible." I guess that was the only part I didn't internalize. I had found a cure for the symptoms, but, not a solution to the problem.

I carried a host of unanswered questions, hatred, and resentment with me. No longer surrounded by forced behavior, principles, rules, and regulations, the confinement was over, and I was in charge of my life now.

I returned home with my guards up, ready for anything my father had in his bag of tricks. He hadn't taken a drink in two years, but, I still didn't trust him, his attitude had not changed. I was nineteen, and I was taken no more shit from him.

CHAPTER 2

IT WAS A WARM SUMMER DAY, when I arrived home from the treatment center. Everybody was out enjoying the weather. I sat on my porch, and surveyed the block; nothing had changed. I saw the same people doing the same thing. Gang members on the corner selling drugs, drug addicts purchasing drugs. The whole scene was depressing, but, at the same time, strangely inviting. I was oddly drawn to the caos. Why it seemed the thugs had the best of everything, I couldn't figure it out. They appeared to be so care free, like they answered to no one.

I watched them everyday, pushing that poison that damn near killed me. Some of my best friends parents were strung out, walking the streets all night like zombies, searching for that temporary cure from the misery that swallowed them up. Their pain stricken faces revealed the wear and tear of years invested in chasing that ghost. It was a sad thing to see.

The most pitiful thing were the women. It was heartbreaking to watch the effect the devil's love potion had on them. Most of them I'd known since I was a kid in elementary school. Now they were in the grips of a demon who had them exploiting their bodies, turning tricks, and neglecting their children. The reality of temptation painted a perfect picture of failure for anyone who dared to believe they were strong enough to beat it! The fight was fixed, and I should've never entered the ring. I was up against a monster who had knocked everybody out in the first round, but not me. I had survived, and was ready to face him again.

CHAPTER 3

I SPENT THE REST OF THE summer hanging out with Cuz. The near death experience I had became a memory, no longer a threat to keep me in line. I was back in the dungeon, getting high everyday. I had learned the lifestyle like a season vet, and Cuz had no problem teaching me the ropes.

We stayed up day and night, everything else came second to getting high. It was the first thing we did when we woke up, and the last thing we did before we went to bed. The more I did, the more I wanted. I was hooked, and it was starting to show.

My appearance was the first thing to go! I wasn't eating, and I was loosing weight five pounds at a time. I was on a crash diet, and crack was the meal. Sometimes, I went days without any sleep or nourishment. It was getting bad, and I still thought I had it all under control.

My mom was devastated! She knew nothing about addiction. She had been through a whirlwind of mental and physical abuse, she was at the end of her rope, and ready to fulfill a promise she had made to herself long ago, she was leaving my father after forty years of marriage.

I tried hard to limit my use, and mask my countenance, but, my attempts were feeble and without merit. I was no match against the mysterious white cloud that delivered me from my situations. Everything I learned in the program, burned to nothing at the end of my torch, traveling through the glass pipe, and evaporating into a puff of smoke. Each hit took with it, a small piece of me.

I kept telling myself, "I was a grown man, it was time I found my own way, and lived my own life." But, the truth was, I had no idea what it took to be a man. I had done pretty much what I wanted to do my whole life, there was no discipline. No one had given me choices, I made my own decisions. My father stayed drunk most of the time, and my mother worked all the time, leaving me to follow the paths of the role models I selected for myself. The streets taught me how to survive. Drug dealers and gang members designed my future, manipulating me at every turn.

I became a product of the hood, and it was open season on the spoil kid from the south side of Chicago.

Being the only child in a household with dysfunctional parents had taken a toll on me from the very beginning. I didn't understand alcoholism, and neither did my mom. I hated my father for years, and I even planned to kill him if he didn't stop attacking us. I kept all that shit bottled up inside me for a long time, scared to share it with my friends. And now, after all these years, she was leaving, and not taking me with her. I felt betrayed, let down, and furiously angry! I was left to face this cruel world without the person who stood by me no matter what, my mom.

I sat at the bottom step of my porch with my faced cuffed in the palm of my hands. Sadness engulfed me, while my mother was in the house packing her bags for the trip to Mississippi. My father sat at the top of the stairs, looking like he wished he could turn back the hands of time, and save his marriage. But, the damage was done, and there was nothing he could do or say to change her mind, he knew he had to let her go.

I looked up at him with fury in my eyes! He was the blame for this, and he knew I hated him for it. For the first time in my life, he avoided eye contact with me, and looked away as I stared him down with vengeance in my heart. Any respect I had for him, left me that very moment. He wasn't my daddy anymore, he was a enemy, and it stayed that way for a long time.

For the next two weeks, we lived together in silence. Mom was gone, and the house wasn't the same. I thought of horrible things to do to him! My anger and hatred grew with each passing day. The bitterness inside me latched out at him in my soul every time I saw his face. I wanted to punish him, I wanted him to feel what I was feeling, and I made it no secret what he'd done to me.

For days I watched him sit on the living room couch, daydreaming about who knows what. He had thrown away forty years of marriage for a drink of whiskey. A part of me wanted to feel sorry for him, but, the memories of everything he'd done overwhelmed any sympathy I could've of possibly had. He was my dad, true enough, but, he was built hard, and I knew he would never apologize for any of the shit he took my mom and I through.

I spent most of my time at the dungeon, getting high, trying to medicate the pain I was feeling inside. As long as I stayed high, I didn't have to think about the drama that surrounded my life. I kept my distance from my father, and buried myself deep in the drug that rescued me. Over and over again, I poured all my problems into that glass pipe. It became that friend I needed. With my mom gone, I became solely depended on it for comfort.

I was young and trapped in a world of destroyed happiness. The circumstances of life had beat me down to the point of surrender, and now I craved a substance unknown to me. My father pulled back, and watched the tiny rock kick in the door of my future. He had spoke of my failure many times in the past, and now he sat back comfortably to watch it become a reality. He feed my craving for crack like a mother breastfeeding a child. I had done nothing to him, and yet he aided me in every wrongdoing. I was becoming more like him in every way. I'd vowed to never duplicate any part of him, or anything that made up the character he was. He had been a like a disease my whole life, and now it had spread throughout me like a virus.

While I was running around, totally outta control, he was planning his getaway back to his hometown, Memphis Tennessee. As much as he hated it, he knew I would have to go with him, and as much as I hated it, I knew it to. Somehow, we would have to learn to tolerate one another, but, how? How could two people with so much common ground find peace? We hadn't found it in 20 years, we surely wouldn't find it now.

I had always wanted a close relationship with my father, but, his drinking always got in the way. He hadn't been abusive my whole life, sometimes he was funny when he was drunk. But, eventually the alcohol took over, and the beast emerged, turning our happy home into a hell above ground!

My father and I spent three days getting ready for our trip to Memphis. As bad as I didn't wanna leave my comfort zone, things were getting outta control, and maybe a change is just what I needed. Maybe I could get a grip on my life before I ended up like Cuz, or worse.

CHAPTER 4

WE LEFT ABOUT TWO O'CLOCK THAT morning. For the first in my life, I would be living somewhere other than where I grew up. Memphis was a familiar place. I spent a lot of time there with my father's parents in my adolescent years. But, the country life wasn't for me, I was a natural born city boy, and I knew this forced geographical change wasn't gonna work for me. I had a plan, and my plan was, to get my mom to move back to Chicago with me and find us an apartment.

The first two weeks in Memphis was hell! I didn't know anybody, and I was craving badly for a hit. I was tempted to comb the neighborhood, and search for the product, but, I had no idea where to start.

From the look of my surroundings, I could tell the love potion had hit Memphis too. It wasn't hard to recognize a person on drugs, they had a unique demeanor that stuck out like a sore thumb. The neighborhood wasn't that much of a difference. The houses were close together, and the block was littered with drug dealers and thugs hanging out on the porches, and sitting on cars.

Watching the dealers on the block reminded me of the caos I'd seen the majority of my life. I thought leaving Chicago would put that lifestyle behind me, but, it was like, stepping outta the furnace and into the fire. It was a different part of the world with the same problems. The drug market was wide open, and families were being destroyed, and taken into custody by that same white cloud that hovered over my neighborhood back home.

I sat on the porch, trying to erase the images in my head, my thoughts drifted swiftly back to those nights at the dungeon, Cuz and I getting high all night, smoking weed, drinking beer and wine, and chasing that ghost. The more I thought about it, the stronger the cravings were. For the first time, since the beginning of this madness, my desire for a hit took precedence over any and everything important.

I went inside, and closed my bedroom door behind me. Fumbling through my wallet, I took out two one hundred dollar bills, and folded them neatly before putting them in my pocket. Now, all I needed to was find the product.

I walked down the block nervously, watching everybody as they stared at me like a stranger in a foreign land. I had never purchased the drugs myself, I'd always left that up to Cuz. But, Cuz wasn't here, and I didn't know how to approach these guys.

I turned the corner at the end of the block, and right in front of me was a group of guys shooting dice in the middle of the streets. "Jackpot!" I said with a low tone, hoping neither of them heard me. "What's up fellas," I said, as I cautiously approached them. They immediately stopped the dice game, and turned toward me. "What you need, weed, crack, what you need?" I couldn't believe it, they didn't even ask who I was. Back in my hometown, there was no way anybody would sell you anything if they didn't know you. You would end up beaten pretty bad, or dead.

I stood there froze! I wasn't sure how to respond, the first thing that came outta my mouth was, "who got the weed?" One of the guys walked away from the crowd and returned with a twenty dollar bag of weed in the palm of his hand. He looked at me strangely, as he handed me the weed and gave me my change for the hundred dollar bill I handed him.

I walked away in the direction of where my father and I lived. I looked back at the guys, as they resumed their dice game. They had just sold to a complete stranger, and not one of them asked who I was, or where I came from.

I made it home, and decided to smoke the weed instead of purchasing the crack. Hopefully it would stop the cravings I was having, and maybe I get high enough to forget about it. I rolled myself a fat ass joint, and sat out in the backyard enjoying the nice weather and solitude that came with the country living.

As the sun went down, my high kicked in, I was so relaxed I didn't even notice it was getting dark. I couldn't move! The weed had me floating, and every muscle in my body had weakened. I remember thinking to myself, "what the f_ _ _ k did I just smoke?" I must have been there for hours, unable to identify with reality. Whatever it was, I dare not smoke the rest of it.

The next day, I woke up in my bed with no recollection of how I got there, my mind was blank; I remembered the high, and nothing else. That would be the last bag of weed I buy in Memphis.

I got myself together, and decided to give my mother a call. My father was totally content with the move, but, not me, I had to get back to the city. I was in a strange city, and the only people I knew were relatives.

I spoke with my mom about the plan I had for us to move back to Chicago, and she agreed as long as my father wasn't coming. She had endured his abuse long enough, and had no intentions of ever mending their marriage, she was done!

A week later, my mom and I were on our way back home, hoping we could start a new life without the drama my father caused. We rode the Greyhound with smiles on our faces, and joy in our hearts. We were finally gonna get that peace we both had been praying for a long time. I didn't have a worry in the world, as long as I had my mom by my side, I didn't need anything else.

CHAPTER 5

MY SISTER PICKED US UP FROM the bus station, and took us to her house. It didn't take long, and within the first week we found a two bedroom apartment on the southside. It was the first time I had ever lived anywhere outside the hood I grew up in. 44th and princeton was where I'd been my whole life.

We moved in the following Friday. It all happened so fast, neither one of us knew what to expect. We spent the entire day getting situated. My mom was so excited! She took her time rearranging the furniture, hanging pictures, fixing up the bathroom, and sitting her plants in the front window to be nourished by the hot sun. It had been a long time since I'd saw my mom smile genuinely. She didn't have to fake it anymore. We assembled our bedroom sets, and took a seat in the living room to watch one of her favorite tv shows, "In the heat of the night."

I sat quietly on the sofa next to my mom, while she was glued to the tv. She seemed so content, and at peace. But, deep inside me, was a demon trying to surface. That same demon that Cuz introduced to me, had followed me, and there was nowhere to run. I was in a big city, and drugs were everywhere!

It had been a while since I got high, and the temptation seemed greater than it ever had before. I didn't know if I should go out and look for it in my new neighborhood, or go back to my old neighborhood.

I went outside and sat on the concrete slab in front of my building, trying to get a feel of my surroundings. It was just like any other ghetto in Chicago, the drug dealers were standing out on the corners selling crack like it was legal. They had addicts coming from every direction, the traffic was non-stop! They were doing it so openly, you'd swear they were paying the police off.

I watched them, trying to select who I would approach. No one seemed to be paying me any attention, until I got up and walked down to the corner. "Hey dude," one of the guys shouted at me! I turned to see which one of them had called me, and before I could figure it out, a short dark completion, rough looking dude stood just two feet in front of me. "What you looking for," he asked with a aggressive tone! I paused briefly before I spoke, not really sure how I should answer him. He opened his right hand, revealing several small folded white packages. "I got dimes," he said in a low tone as if what we were doing was our little secret. My stomach balled up like two fists, as the urge moved through my body demanding the contents of the small packages in his hand. "Give me ten," the words escape my conscious, and rolled of my tongue so quick, I didn't even remember thinking it.

I walked back to my building, and sat back down on the concrete slab. I couldn't get high in the house, there was no way I was gonna let my mother know I was still getting high after that scare I gave her when I had the heart attack. I needed somewhere to get high, that's when I met Disco.

Disco was a young man in his twenties. Short, dark complexion and muscular. He wore long braids in his hair, and his face displayed a rough life. I could see the thug in him, but, not the addict. I would've never made him for a crack head. He wasn't the kind of addict I was used to seeing. He wasn't dingy, and dirty looking like the ones in my hood. His clothes were clean, and he was neatly groomed.

I studied him carefully, as he walked up to the gate that wrapped around the three story building I lived in. He approached me with confidence, as though he knew what my thoughts were. "Whats up dude,' he said, slowly opening the gate, and inviting himself in. I wasn't sure how to react, but, his vibe didn't feel threatening, so I Relaxed and let my guard down. He took a seat on the opposite side of me, and offered a friendly handshake to ease the tension in the air.

"Be careful, don't get to familiar with these shiesty ass cats around here," he warned. "These cats will cross you in a heartbeat!" I didn't know what he saw when he looked at me. Did I really look that venerable, did he see "slow" written across my forehead? The mere fact that he made a statement like that made me wonder what his evaluation of me was. Whether he knew it or not, he would be the main one I'd keep my eyes on.

Disco and I talked for hours, while I tried to figure out his motive for making himself available, and trying to pick me for information about where I'm from, and who I knew. I waited patiently for the conversation I was looking for, and in the next breath, it all came to the surface.

I had seen that look in his eyes from the beginning. Although he didn't look like an addict, he had that same glassy gleam in his eyes I'd saw in Cuz's eyes many times before when he'd been getting high. I took a chance, and asked him the question, "you get high?" He look at me with guilt in his countenance and said, "yeah, do it look that obvious?" I knew he had seen me purchase the dope, and I knew that was his motive for coming over to meet me. Now that the cards were on the table, we could move to the next phase, let's cook this shit and get the party started!

Disco lived only five houses down from me on the same side of the street. It was a run down two flat wood and brick framed home in need of much repairs. The brown paint was chipping badly, and the roof was missing half it's shingles. It looked dark inside, scary and abandoned. There was a dim light coming from the first floor living room of the hideous dwelling. The closer we got to the front door, I could see the light was coming from a lit candle that sat in the center of a broken down in-table. Disco turned the knob and invited me in. I struck my cigarette lighter to light the way, the inside hallway was pitch black. I hesitated before crossing the thresh hole, I didn't know if I was being set up or not. But, something inside me convinced me I could trust him, I followed him in and braced myself for the unknown.

Once inside, I took a seat in a fold up chair I saw near the front door. The rest of the house was so dark, you couldn't see past your hand. The lit candle was the only light in the whole house. I knew all too well what kind of set up this was, it was a trap house. A place where addicts came to ease the pain of their unmanageable lives. A place where they could come and feel accepted, a place where no matter what their situation was, they wouldn't be rejected. It was a erie hole in the midst of a community taken hostage by a hard white substance. It was the second time in my life I'd seen the devastating blow of addiction.

I didn't understand the connection between Disco and his living conditions. He looked to well kept to be living in such terrible circumstances. The whole seen made me wonder if this is how I'm gonna end up if I continued on that path.

We smoked all night, one rock after another, none stop until my heart was beating so loud I could literally hear it as if it were outside my body. The thought of another heart attack crossed my mind, but, was quickly eliminated by another hit of the powerful rock. Disco crawled on all fours, picking up trash that camouflage itself in the dark appearing to him to be crack. I watched him, as the drug took effect on me, forcing me to join him on his journey to insanity. I had seen Cuz in this state many times before, and now I had crossed that line. It was the craziest shit I'd ever done! I couldn't believe it, we had plenty drugs left, and there we were, crawling around on the floor like we had lost our minds.

CHAPTER 6

THAT NIGHT WITH DISCO WAS THE scariest I'd ever experienced. The sun had rose, and I found myself still in the abandoned house wanting more. I knew my mother was probably worried sick not knowing what happened or where I was.

The daylight from the rising sun revealed our previous event. We were dirty and musty, and our eyes were wide open, and bucked like we had seen a ghost! I knew I couldn't go home looking the way I did, my mother would surely know something was wrong. My jeans were falling of me like I had lost weight over night, and all I could think about was another hit.

I had money at home, but, I had no intentions of letting my mom see me this way. The craving got more and more intense, as I sat in the fold up chair trying to map out a plan to get the money. It's amazing the shit you can come up with to deceive someone when you're under the influence of drugs. The lies sound so good, you start believing them yourself.

I was so baffled by the drugs, I didn't even realize how messed up I was becoming. I kept telling myself I was alright, and at the same time, I was lookin throwed away. I reflected back on everything I'd learned at the treatment facility, and tried to put it in the forefront of my mind, but, the drugs were too powerful, and my will had been weakened. I was fully aware of what was happening, but, I couldn't pull back, I was a hostage, and all I could think about was Cuz. I crossed over to insanity, and threw all the tools to recovery away.

Disco left me in the house to go out and hustle for his next fix. I sat in the fold up chair, asking God to sober me up. For the first time in my madness, depression set in, and I felt terrible inside. I knew I had played with fire and got burnt! Reality kicked in as the drugs wore off, and the guilt chewed me up and spit me out with no one there to break my fall. I was in world of shit, and I knew it!

I stared out the front window looking for Disco to return. The drugs had completely worn off, and I needed another hit. I looked around on the floor, hoping one of us had drop something in the darkness. I was losing my mind! The flashbacks of the dungeon with Cuz invaded my memories, and I caught myself picking up everything white. I didn't feel the intense rush from the high, but, I didn't understand why I was trippin so hard.

Again, I thought about the times I'd seen Cuz down on all fours, searching for lost pieces of crack. I thought about how silly he looked, picking up paint chips, drywall, and anything that resembled a rock, trying to smoke it; and now I had reached that point of insanity!

"My God, what am I doing," I shouted aloud, thinking it was the only way he would hear me; and then a strange silence fell over the room, and the paranoia set in. I jumped outta my chair, and ran for the front door. I ran down the block to my house at top speed, looking back to see if anyone was following me. The drugs had me scared shitless, and I hadn't done anything wrong.

I made it to my front door, and took out my keys. I stood there for fifteen minutes, scared to open the door. I knew my mom would be up drinking her morning cup of coffee, surely I didn't want her to see me in this condition. Without warning, she snatched the door open and said, "what's wrong with you, is somebody after you?" I was sweating and my hands were shaking uncontrollably. She had given me the perfect excuse to get my money outta the house. "Yeah moma, I messed up real bad. I've been getting high all night, and I got some stuff on credit. They said, if I don't pay them, they're going to kill me!" It was the first time I'd ever lied to my mother, and I could see the worry in her eyes. She didn't know if I was serious or not, but, she couldn't risk not letting me in. I saw the tears stream down both her cheeks, and she said, "how much Derrick, how much do you owe them?" She stepped aside, and let me in. "Don't worry about it moma, I got it," I replied, with trembling in my voice, trying to sound convincing.

I got the money outta my wallet, and bolted out the door!. Looking back, I could see my mom in the front window watching me as I walked away. She was crushed, scared , and confused.

I made it back to the abandoned house, and let myself in. Disco hadn't got back yet, and I wasn't sure if I wanted to get high by myself. Besides, I didn't see any of the guys on the block selling, and I had no idea where else to go.

I sat in the window, trying to collect myself, and calm down. I had taken my drug usage to the next level. I was acting just like Cuz, strung out, and outta my mind. I hadn't even considered the fact that, not only was I in a strange neighborhood, but, I was sitting in an abandoned house waiting on someone I hardly knew to come back and purchase more drugs for me. I must have been crazy to think I could trust him, but, he was my only link to this madness.

The longer I waited for Disco to return, the more sober I became. The reality of what I was doing, struggled to bring me back to my senses. For the first time since I'd been sitting there, I noticed the rest of the windows in the house were boarded up. The floors were covered in all sorts of garbage. Empty crack bags, and used syringes were all over the floor, and there was an unbearable stinch coming from the rear of the house. I covered my nose, trying to block the foul odor that consumed every room. "Where the hell is Disco," I wondered. As bad as I wanted to leave, I knew I had to stay. The sun was out, and people were starting to move around in the hood. There was no way I was gonna let anyone see me coming outta this place.

Hours passed by, still no Disco. It was beginning to get dark, and I was stuck there. Finally, I was forced to accept he wasn't coming back. The sun had gone completely down, and I knew I would have to come out to purchase it myself.

I waited patiently until one of the dealers passed the house. I tapped on the window, and he looked me directly in my face. He already knew what I wanted, he was the same guy I had bought from the first time.

As he approached the front door, I noticed he had a gun stuffed in the left side of his waist. He opened the door, and walked in with a hand full of folded white packages. "What you need dude," he asked, as he put them on the old coffee table, spreading them out so I could choose. I counted twenty, and said, "I'll take them all!"

I opened three of the packages, and poured them on the table. The cravings hit me harder than ever before. The anticipation of the high rushed through my body like a gentle wind, blowing away all the worthless feelings I had. The drug was my medication, and I desperately needed a dose.

CHAPTER 7

I SPENT THE NEXT TWO YEARS trapped in that white cloud! Any plans I had to better my life were gone. I got high everyday, all day, digging my own grave, one hit at a time. No matter how much I didn't want to admit it, I was addicted, and the pipe was my new best friend.

The horrors of addiction invaded every aspect of my life. I was weak, beaten and broken down. Every attempt to get clean, failed, and the madness progressed rapidly moment by moment. The streets became my number one priority; hustling, stealing, and everything that came with the lifestyle became my occupation.

I had watched Cuz and others in my hood for years being torn apart by this make believe healer. The drugs had swept through my neighborhood demanding souls, and now it was demanding mine. I stood toe to toe with a demon who wouldn.t allow me to escape the nightmare. It was like a never ending dream of the worst kind, and I couldn't wake up! "Had I went to far?" "Was this the bottom the program talked about.?" "How did I get here?" I asked myself these questions repeatedly, never realizing the reality of the answers.

I had become just like the man my father was, only worse. For the second time in my mother's life, she would have to leave someone she loved. Just like my father's drinking, my drug usage had pushed her to the limit. She was mentally, and emotionally broken, and convinced she had failed as a mother. She packed up everything, and went to live with her brother.

The day my mother left was one of the lowest times of my life. I was left to face a world I knew nothing about. The neighborhood had swallowed me up, and left me to suffer the consequences of my choices. I had nowhere to go.

The reality of life on the streets delivered a rude awakening! The abandoned house became my home, and all the misery that came with it, became my only friend. For the first time in my life, I was homeless.

The tools of recovery did nothing to help me regain sanity. The effect of the drugs had washed away any desire I had to change my situation, I couldn't even pray! The guilt was so over-whelming, I hated myself for the mess I'd made of my life.

I spent many nights balled up in a corner of one of the rooms, crying my eyes out, wishing I could turn back the hands of time to the day I knew nothing about cocaine. Everything I saw Cuz go through, was now a part of my life.

I barricaded myself in the house for weeks at a time with no food, electricity, or running water. I had hit bottom so fast, it seemed like it all happened overnight. I remembered the days I used to ask myself, "how something so small, could be so powerful." I didn't have to ask myself the question any more, I was there. I had found my own little dungeon, and I was the landlord.

I pulled the old mirror off the bathroom wall, I couldn't bare the image that looked back at me. My appearance had changed drastically! I wasn't that tall light skinned handsome young man I used to be. I had been tossed to the wolves, and thrown away like a dirty rag. But, I couldn't stop using. The shit was calling me every time I sobered up. It was like a voice inside my head that I couldn't ignore no matter how hard I tried, and all I could do was give in to it's demands.

With each day passing, it got harder and harder to come up with money to get high. My family was outta reach, and no one trusted a word I said. I found odd jobs around the hood to help support my habit, but, that only lasted a couple weeks. Every now and then one of the guys on the block would give me a few bags to sell, and when I got paid, it was mostly in drugs. That only lasted about a month, until I started smoking up the profit.

I kept telling myself, "if I could get outta this neighborhood, maybe I'll get clean. Cocaine was cunning, and baffling; it had a unique way of making you think a geographical change would solve all your problems. But, the truth was, it wasn't the neighborhood that got me high, it was me, and anywhere I went, I took me with me.

The hustling everyday had worn me out! Getting high wasn't fun anymore like it had been in the beginning. The drug wasn't a want anymore, it was a necessity, and I had to have it. I took chances with my life trying to get money to get high. Everybody around me was a victim or a target for my addiction, if you slipped, I got you!

I remember the first time I took a risk that almost got me killed. It was early in the morning, around seven a.m. I had been up all night getting high, and the sun had came up, catching me sitting on the front on the porch. It was a busy morning for the dealers, and they were making money so fast, they got careless, hiding the drugs in plain sight. I watched them like a hawk, waiting for one of them to slip, and finally, opportunity knocked.

The police hit the block from every corner. They scrambled like roaches, throwing bags of crack everywhere. I kept my eyes fixed on one guy, as he ran down the gangway beside me, and stashed his drugs under a old car tire. Disco had just walked up and took a seat next to me, stalking his prey. We waited patiently, as the police cleared the block, and arrested a few of the guys who willing gave themselves up to avoid the beatings from the detectives if they chased you and you got caught.

Disco looked at me and said, "watch my back, I'm gonna get that stash." I watched him walk down the gangway looking for the drugs, but, he walked right past it, and a few feet from the old car tire, he picked up a small brown bag and shook it, only to find out it was empty.

I knew he hadn't saw the stash spot I saw, so, I waited until he came outta the gangway before I made my move. "Damn, the bag was empty," he said in a low tone, trying to keep the conversation between him and I. "I'ma go look down the street, I saw them throw something down by the curb," he said, sounding frustrated.

I went inside and went out the back door of the dungeon, and there it was, sticking out from under the old car tire, "how did he miss that," I wondered. I picked up the bag, and it was full of small white packages. I went back in through the back door, and stashed it in one of the vacant bedrooms under an old dirty mattress. I sat in the fold up chair next to the living room window, and watched the block. My hands were shaking badly at the thought of what they'd do to me if they found out I had gotten the stash.

About thirty minutes had passed, when I heard six loud pops! People started running around the corner to the next block. I quickly got up, and ran in the direction of the crowd. By the time I caught up with everybody, they were all standing in front of the entrance to the building one block over. I walked up, and made my way through the crowd. Disco was lying on the hallway floor with six bullet holes in his head.

I remember thinking, "why did they kill him?" "What had he done so bad to deserve death.?" Then I heard someone say, "he stole the stash, and they saw him coming outta the gangway. My heart fluttered with grief. They had punished the wrong person, I had the stash, and his blood would be forever on my hands.

After Disco's death, I knew my stay in that neighborhood had to come to an end. It would be only a matter of time before they found out who had taken the stash. I had no idea where I was going, but I knew I couldn't stay there.

I went back to the dungeon, and sat there for hours. For the first time since I'd been getting high, the bag of drugs I stashed, meant nothing to me. Disco had lost his life violently, and it was all because of that little white demon.

CHAPTER 8

DISCO'S DEATH DELIVERED A SHOCKING BLOW to the lifestyle I'd chosen. The streets showed no love to the one's trapped by the mystery of the white cloud. The game was cold, and ruthless! The horrors of addiction left only three ends, jails, institutions, and death!

I left the neighborhood a week later with no destination in sight. The image of Disco's body lying in that hallway haunted me everyday. I rode the bus to the east side of the city where my sister lived, hoping she could help me get back into another program. But, when I got off the bus, guilt and shame wouldn't let me reach out for help. I hadn't seen her in two years, and to see her now would tear her apart, my appearance had fell badly.

I sat on the park bench across the street from her building, staring up at her window. The tears flooded my eyes, and I cried harder than I ever cried before. I sat on the bench for hours with my face cuffed in the palm of my hands. I was emotionally destroyed, and I didn't think even crack could mask what I was feeling. I was at the lowest point of my life, and it couldn't possibly get any worse.

The sun had started going down when I saw my sister parking her car, returning home from a long day at work. I wanted to run to her with my arms open wide, but I was too ashamed. I couldn't bring myself to get up off the bench. I kept my head down, hoping she didn't see me. I wanted so desperately to call out her name, but the words wouldn't roll off my tongue. I got off the bench and started walking toward the lakefront. The cool breeze from the lake bounced off the the buildings putting a chill in the night air.

I made it to the lakefront and found a nice clean little spot against a tree, not to far from the water. I took off my jacket and spread it out on the grass. I layed there on my back, looking up at the stars, thinking about all the mistakes I'd made. There I was, lying on the ground, homeless and confused. I thought about the serenity prayer I'd learned in the program. I closed my eyes and recited it aloud; GOD, GRANT ME THE SERENITY TO ACCEPT THE THINGS I CANNOT CHANGE. THE COURAGE TO CHANGE THE THINGS I CAN, AND THE WISDOM TO KNOW THE DIFFERENCE. I asked God to watch over me, as I drifted into a deep sleep.

When I woke up, two days had passed quickly while I was in my comatose like state. It was the best rest I'd had in a long time, and I felt completely rejuvenated. I was sober, and I wanted to stay that way. But, I still needed to do something about my appearance. I was glad I had left the bag of drugs under the old worn out mattress. I was in a new environment, and it felt like a fresh start.

I got up, picked up my jacket, and walked to the nearest store. I went in and stole some soap, razor blades, face towel, and deodorant to tidy up my hygiene. I went in the gas station bathroom, locked the door, and cleaned myself up. My clothes were still dirty, but at least my body was clean.

I stayed sober that entire day. For the first time in two years, my head was clear, and I could think straight. The will to fight my addiction was finally within reach. I began talking to God about my situation, and asking him to deliver me from this madness. But, something inside me wouldn't let me hear his voice. The more I prayed, the more depressed I got. My prayers seem to be in vain, as I struggled to hear a response from God. I had underestimated the power I'd given satan over my life. He was an evil that had no intentions of giving me my life back.

I found myself again on my back, looking up at the stars in deep thought. The devil had crushed my self-esteem, and killed any chance I had of staying sober. I didn't know who to blame, God or myself. I had carried the guilt so long, I needed somebody to dump it on.

I woke up the next morning captivated by my failures. My conscious drenched in shame from the weakness I displayed as a man. My strength misdirected, and placed in the grasp of the devil's love potion. The urges came with force, as I stood to my feet, shaking the grass and leaves of my jacket. I needed to get high! The bad memories were pushing me to the thought of suicide, and I couldn't shake the progression of the demon. He was powerful, cunning, and baffling, and I had made him god over my life. Tricked and deceived by his works, I was a soldier in his army of delusional happiness.

I walked away, looking back at the still water that surrounded my little home beside the tree. I had seen death, and now there was only two ends left; jails and institutions, and I was knocking at the door of mental instability.

CHAPTER 9

THE EASTSIDE WASN'T ANY DIFFERENT THAN any other side of Chicago. It was infested with drugs, gangs, drug addicts, and every other low-life you could think of. It was once known for it's wealth and beautiful scenery, but, just like the rest of the city, the devil's love potion had swept through their neighborhoods too.

The dealer's sat on the park benches, smoking weed, drinking beer, and selling drugs in broad daylight, out in the open. "Damn, this shit is everywhere," I thought to myself, as I passed them cautiously, looking back, taking a mental picture of everyone I saw.

I was standing on the corner, getting ready to cross the street when I heard someone say, "hey dude, check it out." I turned around, and there was a young man approaching me, walking at a fast pace. I didn't know if I should run, or wait to see what he wanted. The traffic light changed, and I was stuck there to face him. "Hey dude, you wanna work," he said, looking me up and down, as if he knew I was an addict. It was no secret he as a drug dealer, I'd seen him on the park benches with the rest of the guys, and his dress code was a dead give away. They all wore, baseball caps, blue jeans, white t-shirts, and Jordan's. "Take a walk with me," he said as the light changed, and we both crossed the street.

We walked a couple of blocks over, and ended up in front of this huge three story brick building. The block looked well kept, the grass neatly groomed, the sidewalks clean, and litter free except, for a few potato chip bags here and there.

The building looked quiet and deserted. I could see curtains in the front window of the first floor apartment, but, no activity. The second and third floor apartment windows were covered with newspaper.

"They call me Cotton," the young man said, snapping me outta my deep thought about taking another step. "They call me Red," I replied, watching every move he made. We walked down the gangway next to the building, and entered the first floor apartment through the back door.

The apartment was clean, and strangely quiet. I expected something or someone to jump out at us at any given second! The place was completely unfurnished, except for a old sofa, and a twenty one inch color t.v. that sat on two red milk crates. "Take a look around, get familiar with the place," he said. "Take a look around," I thought to myself, the place was empty, there was nothing to get familiar with.

He reached under the old sofa, and pulled out a small fold up table, and a round mirror about the size of a dinner plate. He reached in the front of his pants, and removed a plastic bag containing hundreds of small white packages.

He explained his business in detail to me, over and over and over again, making sure there was no miscommunication about what I was suppose to do. I sat there, fondling with the thought of changing my mind. I knew nothing about this dude, or what he was capable of if something went wrong. I was an addict, addicted to the very substance he wanted me to sell, there was no way this would end up good.

Why had he chose me?. I was a new face, in a new area, a complete stranger, and homeless. Why did he trust me? Was this a blessing, or a curse? For a moment, I didn't even think about the drugs. I wouldn't have to sleep in the park anymore, at least that problem was solved.

I watched him, as he walked out the back door, handing me a key, and locking it behind him. I stared at the plastic bag on the small table. The bag was full of small white packages, stuff with tiny pebbles of crack. I counted them slowly, and carefully, making sure I didn't make a mistake. 5, 10, 15, 20, I kept going until the count ended at 200! "Damn," I said out loud! I put the drugs under one of the seat cushions on the old sofa, and got up to take a tour of the place, making sure no one else was in there. The bedrooms were dark, and had no light bulbs or beds in them. The bathroom was clean, and smelled like cherry incense, but, no light bulb. I opened the kitchen drawer, and found five yellow candles I knew would come in handy once the sun went down. I was in a trap house, with no one to watch my back but me. It was an unfamiliar place, and I was sure the police knew of it's activities. The images of the doors being kicked in, scared me stiff for a moment, as I made my way to the living room window to look out for any impending danger. I had really put myself in harm's way this time. I was an addict, and even I knew monkey's can't sell bananas.

The longer I sat there, the more I wanted to recant the decision I'd made to work for Cotton. I had never sold drugs before, and I definitely couldn't be successful at it know, I was using.

I watched the block like a hawk, taking a mental picture of everyone I saw, even police that circled the neighborhood in unmarked cars, dressed in plain clothes. The addicts weren't hard to notice, their appearance gave them away. The dingy look, dirty clothes, and suspicious behavior always revealed their intentions. It was weird how the drug seem to affect everyone the same way. I had been using for over two years now, and I hadn't met anyone who could stand up to the powerful punch it packed! There was some who tried to maintain a manageable life while using, but, eventually they ended up just like the rest of us, lost and turned out.

I watched the addicts come out of their hiding places. The darker it got, the more of them I saw. They were like roaches when the lights went off. They were all over the block, looking to purchase that temporary relief from insanity, and I had the cure.

They walked down the gangway in a single file line, headed to the back door. By the time I got to the door, they were waiting with money in their hands. I served them all, one at a time. As fast as I cleared the porch, it would fill up again in seconds! The two hundred bags were gone within an hour. I had sold everything he gave me.

I needed to call him, and the nearest pay phone was a block away. I wasn't sure if I should stash the money, or carry it with me. I had a thousand dollars in my hand, and I needed to get it to him quick! The cravings came instantly, as I locked the back door, stuffing the money in my pocket.

As soon as I cleared the gangway, I was met by one of the people I'd served. A thin black girl in her mid thirties stood in front of me. "Whats up man," she said. I could see the glass stem cuffed tightly in her left hand. "Whats up with you," I replied. "Nothing, just trying to see if you wanna get into something, I need a hit." It was the first time I had ever been approached like that. I had my limitations, there was a point in which I drew the line, and she had just crossed it. I felt bad for her, she was craving bad for a hit. "Is there somewhere we could go to get high," I asked? The words barely rolled off my tongue, "hell yeah," she said, with a big smile on her face.

I followed her to the end of the block we were on, to another three story brick building that was totally condemned. The front of the building was boarded up with thick sheets of plywood tagged, "NO TRESPASSING!" She looked at me with security in her eyes, hoping to elude any doubt I may have had of entering the building. "How we gonna get in," I asked, with concern in my voice. She pointed to the back of the building down a long and dark gangway. I knew, in a normal state of mind, there was no way I'd take such a risk. But, the urge to get high took a front row seat to any fear I had about entering the building.

It was obvious she had been there before. "Come on," she said, reaching for my hand to lead me down the long dark gangway. I followed her cautiously, looking behind me, watching my back, and bracing myself for the unknown.

Behind the building, was a small fenced in area, and a old car that looked like it had been set on fire. A stack of old car tires served as steps that lead to the back door. The thick plywood had been torn down at the rear entrance of the building. She climbed the tires carefully until she made it to the top. She was a pro, and you could tell she had plenty practice.

She walked through the entrance to the building, and her image blended in with the darkness. I could her her footsteps, as she moved through the trash and filt, kicking beer cans and wine bottles outta her way. "Hey dude," she called out, "come on in." I climbed the tires easily to my surprise, and stepped into the darkness, putting my hands out in front of me to guide my way. I struck my lighter to illuminate my surroundings. The building was a mess! It was cluttered with old pissed out mattresses, and box springs. Dirty clothes, broken dishes, and old gym shoes were scattered everywhere. A horrible odor of urine, and feces claimed the fresh air that blew in from the outside. It was the worst conditions I'd ever seen! But, little did I know, I would become the landlord of this dreadful place.

The thin black girl cleared out a spot in the bedroom near the back door, and lit a candle she had in her purse. I sat down on a milk crate, and tried to regain my sanity. I hadn't even attempted to contact Cotton to give him his money, and I was sure he would be looking for me shortly. I wasn't high yet, and I still had time to make the right decision, but, I was broke, and the only way I was gonna get high, I had to spend his money.

CHAPTER 10

I HAD NO WAY OF KNOWING when Cotton would be looking for me, nor did I know who had seen me that knew him. The paranoia started to set in, as I sat quietly watching the thin girl waiting for me to present the drugs. She was feigning badly, looking at me with her eyes bucked like they were gonna pop outta their sockets!

I wanted to get high just as bad as she did, but, all I had was money, and I had no idea where to get it from, I would have to trust the thin girl. I reached in my pocket, and handed her a fifty dollar bill, her face lit up like christmas tree! "I'll be right back," she said, bolting out the back door!

It seemed like forever, while I waited for the thin girl to return. I paced back and forth through the dim lit apartment, hoping Cotton wasn't on the hunt for me, and his money. I was extremely nervous, and my hands were shaking like leaves on tree. I watched the back door, trying to focus in the darkness that surrounded me. I couldn't see a thing, and suddenly, an image appeared in the rear entrance of the building. Blinking my eyes rapidly, I could only hear the footsteps of the unidentified figure fast approaching me. "Who is that," I yelled out! "It's me," she replied, and a sudden rush of ease fell over me, as she stepped into the room exposed by the candle light.

I was so glad to see her, I didn't even care if she had the drugs or not. I was just glad I didn't have to be in that scary ass building alone.

We stayed barricaded in the condemned building for two days. We boarded up the back door with an old piece of plywood. We were so high and paranoid, we didn't realize we had trapped ourselves inside. We had closed up the only exit to the outside.

As the sun set for the second time, the high began to wear off, and the candle had burned completely out. We were in total darkness, I couldn't see my hand in front of my face. The thin girl sat quietly, as her image disappeared in the darkness. I could hear her breathing, but, I couldn't see her. "What we gonna do now," she asked? I didn't have clue, I had blown the whole thousand dollars, and the only thing on my mind was, getting the hell outta that neighborhood.

A strange silence engulfed the apartment. It felt like something or someone was lurking in the dark, waiting to pounce on us, when all of a sudden, "BOOM!" The plywood hit the floor with a loud thump! "I know you in here!" I put my hand over my mouth tightly, trying to muffle the sound of my breathing. "Where the f_ _ _ k is my money," he shouted, as the voice got closer and closer. The thin girl sat quietly, and didn't move a muscle. She was innocent, and knew nothing of what I'd done, and now her life was being threatened for something she had nothing to do with.

In a desperate attempt to clear her name, the thin girl screamed out, "he's in here!" The footsteps got closer, as they followed the sound of her voice, until they were standing over me, striking a lighter to see. Cotton looked me dead in the eye and said, "if you ain't got my money, you gonna die!" It was three of them. Before I could get up, one of them hit me in the jaw so hard, it knocked me backwards of the milk crate. I cuffed my face with both hands, trying to protect my eyes. The blows came swiftly, and punishing without mercy. They dragged me out into the back yard, and stomped me. I balded up in a fetal position, covering my head. But, it was no use, every blow found its mark, while my hands covered themselves in blood. In outta nowhere, I felt the painful thump of a baseball bat connect with my head, and just like that, I was out cold!

They took me to the building where the drugs were sold, tied my hands behind my back, and bound my feet together. I was returning to consciousness, when I heard one of the guys say, "where's the money?" Both of my eyes were swollen shut, I couldn't see a thing. The pain from the beating, raced through my body, while I laid on the floor in silent prayer. I tried to lie still, hoping they would think I was dead. But, mercy wasn't an option, the beatings resume with forceful blows of the baseball bat, striking my ribs, back, and legs; and as fast as the beatings begin, everything stopped. I heard the door close, and suddenly, all was quiet.

The next day, I woke up in the emergency room, badly beaten with no recollection of how I got there. I was just glad to be alive.

CHAPTER 11

FOR THE SECOND TIME IN MY life, I'd been face to face with death! The horrors of addiction were more real to me than ever before. I had been beaten within an inch of my life, and for what, a feeling? Someway, somehow, I had to stop this madness. But, the drug had a hold on me, and deep down inside, I knew I wasn't finish.

I stayed in the hospital for two weeks, battling the wounds that had been afflicted by Cotton and his boys. They had put a beaten on me I'd never forget. I knew I would see him again, I had nowhere else to go. Although, my sister didn't know I was in her area, I felt better being close to her, even if she didn't know it.

I had no idea what happened to the thin girl, I could barely remember the attack on my life. I remembered the drug house, and the vacant building, but everything else was a blank. But, one thing was very true, it did happen, because I was sore as hell, my body purple, blue, and severely bruised. There wasn't a spot on my body that didn't receive punishment.

After being discharged from the hospital, I went back to the hood looking for Cotton. I had to make good with him on the money I owed him. I didn't wanna spend the rest of my life looking over my shoulder, and besides, I wasn't accustomed to running no matter what the risk were.

The block was cluttered with its usual activities, addicts looking to score, drug dealers pushing the product, and the police waiting for one of them to slip. I sat at the bus stop across the street to keep outta sight. From where I sat I could see Cotton if he pulled up with his goons by his side.

He was a little dude, about five feet, nine inches tall; dark skinned, in his mid twenties, weighing about a hundred and twenty pounds soak and wet. On a normal day, I would'a beat the shit outta him, but, it didn't take much strength to pull a trigger, and where I was from, guys like him always carried a gun.

I hadn't really taken a good look at the damage they did, but, I could feel the puffiness around my eyes. I got up to look at my reflection in the window of the parked car in front of me, I looked disfigured! There was no way I was gonna let him and his goons get away with beating me like that, even if I was wrong. My face was messed up, and I was pissed off!

I sat at the bus stop, thinking about going back to my neighborhood, and rounding up my guys. I knew goons to, but, I wasn't sure if I could depend on them now that I had a drug problem. Being on drugs meant people looked at you different, no one respected addicts where I came from. My neighborhood was full of them, and I saw how they were treated.

Minutes later, I saw Cotton pull up in front of the building driving a white cadillac with custom wheels on it. The chrome flickered each time he turned the tires, placing it perfectly against the curb. He got out, surveyed his surroundings, and went inside the building. "Damn, he by himself," I said in a low tone. It was a perfect opportunity for revenge! I had him at a grave disadvantage, and I knew I could return punishment. He deserved to die for what he'd done to me, he and his goons had left me for dead.

I looked around on the ground by the bus stop for a weapon; anything I could use to afflict pain. Five feet to the left of me, was a broken wooden bat. I picked it up, and put in the small of my back, and pulled my t-shirt over it to cover it up. I crossed the street with fury in my eyes! He had no idea I was coming, and I intended to wear the bat down to a nub beating his ass!

I crept down the gangway with the bat gripped tightly in my right hand. I found a secluded little spot under the stairs in the rear of the building. I picked up an old blue milk crate, and sat down , waiting patiently for him to come out. I was gonna get my revenge by any means necessary! I had to show him what the element of surprise felt like.

I sat there for hours waiting on him to come out. The sun had set, and the darkness covered me, consuming my position even deeper in the night. A sprinkle of moonlight broke through the hidden clouds, and lit up the rear entrance to the building, making it easier to see him when he came out.

Finally, I heard a click, as he turned the lock, opening the back door. "This is it!" I said mentally, as I stood up, and positioned myself for attack. Cotton locked the back door, and walked down the steps, gripping his nine millimeter in his left hand. "Damn," I thought quietly, "he got a gun." He hesitated before facing the gangway, as if he knew something or someone lurked in the pitch darkness.

I stood quietly, as he began to walk in my direction, holding my breath to muffle the sound of my lungs expanding. He walked past me without a clue that I was there. I sprung out of the darkness, swinging the broken bat violently at his arm. The bat connected with extreme force, breaking his arm, as the gun fell to the ground. He scrambled frantically, trying to recover the weapon; but it was too late. In one rapid motion, I picked up the gun, stuck it in the small of my back, and swung again, this time striking him in the center of his stomach. His body went limp, as he grasp for air, hitting the ground like dead weight!

I continued my assault with deadly vengeance! All I could think about was what he'd done to me. The memories fueled my anger, and I beat him furiously until I couldn't swing anymore. I dropped the bat, and took a few steps back to see if he was still alive. He wasn't moving, but, I could hear him groaning. I had beat him within an inch of his life, and now he would be left for dead.

I creeped outta the gangway the same way I'd creeped in, quietly, and cautiously. I had gotten my revenge. I stepped outta the darkness, and revealed myself under the street lamps. Walking away slowly, I thought to myself, "where do I go from here."

CHAPTER 12

ABOUT THREE MONTHS HAD PASSED BY since my attack on Cotton. I had given him a ass whoopin he'd never forget, and no one knew it was me.

My wounds had healed completely, and surprisingly, there were no scars. I found another abandoned building about four blocks away from the trap house, and settled in.

The building was similar to the last one, except for the running water. It was a three story red brick building with six units. It too was abandoned, and all of the windows were broken out. The brick was chipping from years of wear and tear.

Every room in the building was demolished! Holes in the walls, ceiling caving in, installation exposed, and the hardwood floors were cracking, leaving huge holes in the floors. For now, I convinced myself it would be ok to squat there, considering it was still warm outside. But, the winter months were only days away, and there was no way I'd be able to live there in the cold.

I wanted desperately to call on my family. I had backed myself in a corner, facing horrible living conditions. The pressure mounted, giving me a terrible migraine headache, my temples pulsating with pain. No one had seen me for over two years, and I wondered if anyone cared.

The depression of addiction had me at my lowest, and everyday I contemplated suicide. I sat in the ruins of my dungeon, replaying my life, trying to mentally grasp the old me. The me that had great plans for his life. The me that wanted to serve God, and preach his word. Somewhere deep in my soul, I knew my will to serve God still existed. I could hear his voice somewhere in the far distance of my spirit, calling me to repentance. My heart bleed, and my eyes webbed up with tears, as I sat there with my hands stretched over my head. I pleaded with God for a way outta this mess I was in. I was weak, beaten and defeated by the adversary I had given charge over my life.

I was talking to God audibly, hoping he was listening. I don't know what I expected him to do if I wasn't ready. My body fought against every prayer I submitted, openly crying out for another hit. I needed God to move now, I needed him to hear me now, as I shouted out his name. I needed that God my mom, and grandparents talked about when I was growing up. He was near, I could feel him, but my addiction pushed him away, holding me hostage to a demon I was powerless against.

I could hear the rats stirring around in the dungeon. The reality of where I was surfaced, snapping me outta my visit with God. The powerful deception of addiction took over, and sent me back behind that door to freedom from its boundage. I could only peek in, and see what life used to be like. The force that held me back, took me prisoner to its demands. God was the answer, and I knew it, but, my ears couldn't comprehend his instructions, nor was my body a willing vessel.

This was the bottom I'd seen Cuz swallowed up in. It had taken him years to reach total submission to his addiction, but, for me it seemed as though it all came crashing down over night! Just two years of drug abuse, and I was there, a twin to the pain that Cuz lived, and misery became my roommate. I had my own dungeon now, and I was the landlord.

CHAPTER 13

THE WINTER MONTHS SET IN, AS the temperature began to drop to a blistering ten below zero. I had found a dealer only one block over from where I squatted, which made it easy for me to sneak outta the rear of the dungeon, and score without being seen.

I spent the daylight hours, standing in front of the local restaurant asking for change, and hoping my sister didn't ride by and see me out there. It was humiliating, and the most embarrassing thing I'd ever done.

The panhandling was my only source of income, and each day I woke up to face another fight, I submitted to my low self esteem and did what I had to to exist. It became my job, and I went to work faithfully everyday. Some gave, and some didn't, but, I stood there committed until I had what I needed to feed my body, and my addiction.

It was strange how convinced I was about my situation. It was as if I never knew another life before drugs. The more I used, the more it seemed it had always been that way. It was like my past life didn't exist, and the good old days were a dream that never came true.

As crazy as it may sound, I became oddly comfortable living the lifestyle that had been introduced to me. I was far beyond blaming anyone else for my involvement, I made the choices, and I was responsible for my current circumstances. Cuz wasn't there putting the pipe in my hand, I was picking it up with my own free will, constantly telling myself, "this is my last hit."

The twelve steps and twelve traditions of narcotics anonymous were a part of me, but, they were no match against the demon that dwelled in me, and a will governed by a white cloud of false hope. I was on trial, fighting for my sanity, and the only counsel I had in my defense, was me.

CHAPTER 14

IT WAS A SLOW DAY, AS I made my way back to the dungeon, disappointed and hungry. It was a bitter cold night, and the hustle only accumulated enough money to do either or. I decided to walk down the alleys instead of being out in the open. The rumor was out that Cotton was looking for me, but, for what? I knew he didn't see me the night I beat him damn near to death, and I hadn't told anyone about what I'd did.

I stopped at the dealer, purchased the product, and made my way to the dungeon. It started to snow, while I closed the back door, placing two milk crates against it so I could hear if anyone tried to come in. It was the only security I had to keep from being surprised by strangers.

Usually, I would sit in the corner of one of the vacant bedrooms, and use the moonlight to see what I was doing. But, this night it was bitter cold, and the snow was blowing through all the broken windows, confining me to the small area I was sitting in. The candle I had wouldn't stay lit, the wind was too strong. I took my coat off, and put it over my head, holding the pipe in my hand, I hit it, inhaling deeply until the glass was clear of any trace of the white cloud. I exhaled with force, blowing out the smoke, as it mixed with the blowing snow, camouflaging itself in the cold winter air. The high took effect immediately, and the beat of my heart echoed through my open mouth loudly like the sound of a drummer out of rhythm. I stood straight up, unable to move from the potency of the tiny pebbles. My heart thumping louder and louder, as I struggled to put one foot in front of the other. "I gotta get outta here," I kept telling myself, but, my body wasn't responding. The hit had me petrified, and stiff, as it traveled through my system, forcing me to brace myself against the wall behind me. "Someone is coming," I thought to myself! The drugs increased my hearing, while I pinned myself in the corner of the room, facing the darkness. It was all in my head, there was no one there but me.

Finally, the grip of the powerful hit released me, as the winter wind whipped through the broken window, forcing me outta the room, out of the darkness, and into the stream of moonlight that beamed in. I stood in the center of the floor, watching the back door, anticipating danger on the other side. The paranoia was too much for me to bare. I removed the milk crates from in front of the door, and opened it. There was no one there but me.

That night was one of the craziest experience I'd ever had. Being alone in a abandoned building was hard to get used to. I wasn't the only addict who went there to use, but, I was the only one who had decided to move in during the coldest season of the year.

It was a brutal winter, and it caught me at one of the lowest times in my life. I was homeless, and addicted to a substance that had damn near ran me crazy! I had lost a lot of weight, and my appearance had changed dramatically. My will to regain my sanity had been defeated at every attempt to fight. I needed help, but, didn't have the strength to accept it, or ask for it.

Deep down inside, I knew I had to change my life. The memories of the person I used to be, and the person I wanted to be, sometimes flashed before my eyes. I wanted to be set free from my mental, and emotional boundage. "If I could only have the high without the consequences, everything would be alright," I kept trying to convince myself. My level of sanity was no match for my current circumstances, I was outta my mind to think I could keep getting high, and be successful in life. But, that was the cunning part of addiction, the more I used, the more I thought I could be a functioning addict. Although my actions had proved that to be an impossible task, I never stopped entertaining the thought.

The winter had beaten me down to a pitiful representation of a man. I was about, a hundred and thirty pounds, skin and bones, and still hadn't accepted my defeat. The only living friend I had, was a tiny black kitten that used to crawl under the old covers I had, and tuck himself under my arm each night, and we would wake up several mornings covered in snow.

I never knew where the kitten came from, but, I believed for some divine purpose, It was an Angel sent by God to watch over me.

CHAPTER 15

AS THE COLD WINTER MONTHS VANISHED in the warm spring sun, the leaves covered the trees with a beautiful green. It had been a while since I noticed the beauty of nature. Everything looked bright, and refreshing, as I stood up and folded the covers, stacking them neatly in the corner of the stairway.

I was sober, and now would be the perfect time to keep away from that first hit. I walked outta the building, standing in the middle of the alley, I raised my hands above my head, and in a brief worship I said, "thank you Father for waking me up safe and unharmed." I had survived another blistering winter, addicted or not, I knew I hadn't done it on my own.

It was strange how God watched over me in my sin. He had been there from the very beginning of this horrible nightmare. The difficulties of addiction had taken all of the fun outta gettin high, and now it had become a matter of life and death.

I made my way to my usual spot in front of the local restaurant. I was broke, and weak from lack of nourishment. I stood there for an hour, begging for change until I had enough for french fries and a pop. I hadn't eaten in a about two days, the fries were so good, I thought I was eating a T-Bone steak!

I licked my fingers lustfully, trying to savour the flavor of the mild sauce, when all of a sudden, I saw my sisters car pulling into the parking lot where I stood. The tires screeched, as she came to an abrupt stop right in front of me. I could see my brother on the passenger side, with a angry look on his face! I thought about running, but, my legs wouldn't move, and I didn't have the energy anyway.

The passenger side door flung open! My brother got out with his fist balled up, and walked straight up to me, and grabbed me by both shoulders, pulling me until we were face to face, he said. "What the f_ _ _k is your problem, you about to run momma crazy, we been looking for you for two years!" "Get your ass in the car," he shouted, his eyes bloodshot red with anger!

I climbed in the back seat without hesitation. My sister turned to look at me, and the tears streamed down her cheeks, as she pulled outta the parking lot into traffic.

A warm sense of relief washed over me, while I sat quietly in the back seat, hoping I wouldn't get drilled with a thousand questions. I had no idea where we were going, and at that moment, I didn't care. They had found me, and rescued me from me.

After about thirty minutes on the expressway, things started to look familiar. My mom had landed a job with a rich white man, and moved to Lake forest, and we were headed in that direction. I didn't want my mom to see me messed up like this, but a part of me needed to feel her embrace. She was the only one who hadn't completely turned their back on me.

My mom and I had been through a lifetime of pain and misery at the hands of my father's abuse. It had took her forty years to find her peace and mind, and there I was bringing it back to reality. She deserved to be left out of the mess I'd made of my life.

My sister drove right past the exit to my mother's house, and now I was really confused, I didn't have clue where we were going, and the only place I knew in that direction was the Lake County Jail. I had been arrested for possession a few years back, and had missed court.

"We want you to turn yourself in," my sister said, emotionally broken. The look on my sister's face went all through me. I watched the tears roll down her cheeks, as she pleaded with me to do the right thing. That demon reared up his ugly head, trying to dismiss my sister's plea. But, I was tired and broken. The two year run had gotten the best of me, I needed the rest.

I agreed to the request, as we pulled up in front of the jail. I had every intention of going in and surrendering to the sheriff, but just as I was about to get outta the car, my brother handed me a fifty dollar bill and said, "put this on your books for commissary." I took the money and got outta the car, and went inside. It was the worst thing he couldn't ever did for me. I took a seat, waiting for the sheriff to escort me to central booking, but the cravings had began, and there was no way I'd turn myself in now.

I wasn't totally captivated, there was still a small part of me that wanted to stay, but the sheriff was taking to long, giving me too much time to think, something I had failed to be good at. I got up, and went outside to smoke, when I noticed my sister's car was gone.

I tried hard to stay put, but the cravings were too strong! I ran to the metra train station as fast as I could, and caught the first train to Lake Forest. The ride took about twenty minutes. I stared out the window, admiring the beautiful scenery, as the train pulled into the station. It was in the middle of the day, and people were coming and going by the dozens.

I dropped my head, walking past them like I was invisible, hoping no one would get an eye full of my presence. I was a mess, and there was nothing I could do to mask my appearance.

I found the public bathroom, and went inside locking the door behind me. I had already called my mom, and asked her to meet me at the station, which was only about a twenty minute walk from her house. I wasn't in the bathroom ten minutes before someone knock on the door. "Who is it.? I said, in a soft tone, trying not to sound suspicious. I opened the door, "put your hands up!" Yelled the white man, neatly dressed in a two piece suit. "Lake County Sheriff," he shouted! "Is your name, Derrick Turner," he asked? There was no denying who I was, I was an exact match to the photo he held in his hand. He cuffed my hands behind my back, and escorted me outta the station and into the back seat of his cruiser.

On my way to jail, I thought about all the mistakes I made, and all the people I had hurt, the guilt was overwhelming! I had never seen my sister cry, nor had I ever seen my brother that angry. I had let everybody down, including myself. I had big dreams for my life, and drugs had crushed them all.

CHAPTER 16

I SPENT EIGHTEEN MONTHS IN THE county jail before I was released. My stay there was long and confined. I had gained my weight back, and my appearance improved immaculately! I was the new Derrick on the outside, but, the inside was still lacking the strength to change.

The day I got discharged was a confusing experience. I was glad to be free, but, I was not ready to face life on life's terms. That demon in me stirred up my spirit as soon as I saw daylight. I couldn't believe it. After all that time I spent behind bars, you would think the desire to use again would be gone. But no, it was still there, stronger than ever before. It was like an outer body experience, one body waited patiently on the outside, until the incarcerated body connected to it.

I moved in with mom in the rich white man's house, it was huge. The front lawn was the size of a football field. The driveway was long, and laced on each side of it, were beautiful tropical trees in bright red, green, and purple colors. There was a three car garage with parking space for visitors.

The mansion had twelve bedrooms, ten bathrooms, and a large enclosed sun porch with a variety of small trees and beautiful flowers, a perfect place for solitude and peace.

I really tried hard to adjust to my new life in the wealthy suburb, taking long walks with my mom in the warm summer sun. We made plans to visit other parts of the world, like Italy, Paris, Hawaii, Jamaica, California, and Las Vegas. During our walks, I watched her smile, and for the first time in a long time, it was genuine, she didn't have to fake it to hide the pain inside. I loved my mom more than life itself, but, there was still a part of me that held a deep resentment towards her. She had improved her life, and left me behind to face the evil that lived in my dad.

We woke up every morning, and planned our day at the breakfast table. I was happy for her, but, my addiction had changed me into this bitter, and numb person. The pipe was calling me, as if it had an audible voice. I woke up many nights, feeling like I had gotten high in my dreams. The urges were strong, and demanding, and each day I was getting closer and closer to relapse. I had no idea where my addiction would take me this time, but fighting it was not an option. I had a Gorilla on my back, and he was about to break free.

I didn't understand how I could entertain the thought of getting high after all I'd been through. The circumstances were real, and the memories were vivid, and yet I wanted another hit.

I thought about Cuz many times during my mental relapse. I thought about his condition, and his insanity, in which, now I'd come to know so well. My mind wondered, but my body was present, while I walked through the beautiful neighborhoods of the wealthy suburb with my mom. She had no clue of the plans I was making to relive my nightmares. I had mentally sold my soul again to the white cloud, and it would be a struggle that nearly drove me to suicide!

CHAPTER 17

MY STAY IN THE WEALTHY SUBURB was short lived after I made my way back to the city. I dove right back in my mess like I had never left it. I went back to my neighborhood, and continued the chase with Cuz. The block didn't feel the same, my mother and father had gone their separate ways after a long stressful and abusive marriage.

Staying with Cuz was another one of my bad choices, but I had nowhere else to go. Seeing my old house everyday only added to the pain I concealed deep inside. The memories of the good old days haunted me everyday.

I could see the hatred in the eyes of people who had known me all my life. It was like they waited for me to fall, and they enjoyed watching me shatter my dreams.

Living with Cuz was like being trapped in a house fire, everywhere you looked, there was smoke. The traffic in and out all night long, was nerve wrecking! Everyday was the same routine; get up, get high, get more, get high, it never stopped. It went on and on, and sometimes we went days without food or sleep.

I spent the next three years confined to Cuz's little dungeon. My mother was totally distraught, and at the point of an emotional break down. I hated myself for the misery I was putting her through, But, I kept telling myself that I was the only one suffering. It was twice as bad as it was the first time around, I fell off quickly.

My family tried everything to get me out of that self made hell! But, the cunning and baffling character defects of my addiction, ran circles around them. They believed every lie I could come up with to swindle them outta money. I got so good at deception, I started believing the lies myself.

I was a crook of the worst kind, and nobody trusted me. But, I wasn't a fool, I knew if I didn't stop what I was doing, it would surely get me hurt or maybe even killed! Some off the chances I took to get high, were insane! The drugs sent me off like a blind man in the midst of a pack of wolves. I had to have it, and if you had it, you had to give it up.

Getting high became a way of life for me. It was the only thing that listened to my cries, it was the only thing that felt my pain, it was my way out of the insanity, even if it only freed me for a short while. But, I wasn't the only one. My old neighborhood reminded me of a zombie movie, especially at night. The crack had destroyed some of the best individuals. People I knew that had promising careers before that demon sunk his claws in them. They walked the streets all night chasing that first hit. The men robbed and stole anything of value to feed that craving, while the women sold their bodies for that feeling that held them hostage.

Cuz's house became the den for that temporary relief from insanity. It was a place we all went to pour out our troubles, and surrender our pain. We were infected with a disease that we could only fully recover from in death.

CHAPTER 18

EACH DAY OF MY LIFE I carried the weight of my failures. I had become a menace to my own mind, terribly driven to the point of suicide. I had been a momma's boy all my life, but I lacked the skills it took to be a man. I was left to face this cruel world all by myself, and no one prepared me for it.

My brother was a perfect example of what it took to be a man. He tried hard to install his qualities in me, but, the bright lights of the ghetto life drew me in like a fish on a hook, and I took refuge in all the wrong things, and in the blink of an eye, I became wasted talent.

It was no use crying now, the damage was done. My hard head had made a soft ass, and I was at war with my own mind. I'd forgotten how to roll with the punches and dodge the blows, and that demon in me connected with each swing. I had been dealt a cruel hand, and every card I played was to my disadvantage.

I was surrounded by those who envied me my whole life. They hid behind fake smiles, and phony conversation. They were back stabbers, looking for a soft place to stick the knife. My father taught me about people like this, but, my desire for drugs clouded my judgement. I was so blinded by the devil's love potion, I couldn't see past my hand.

Covered in the darkness of my addiction, I felt completely disabled, and torn apart by the insanity that came with my incurable disease. I was hypnotized by the feeling that came with each hit, until the fight in me was no more. I was a drug addict, bound by the horrible terms and conditions that came with the contract I signed, giving it charge over my life.

Each day it got harder and harder to support my habit. I had burned my bridges with my family, and all the lies caught up with me. Nobody answered their phones when I called, and nobody bothered to look for me. The depression was unbearable, and the guilt sent me chasing the high even more.

All the things I learned in the program tried to play a role in my destruction, but, my will was to weak, and I loved the high more than the fight to change my life. Any desires I had to achieve my goals, were put on hold against the feeling I got from the white cloud. There was no looking back now, I couldn't see the glory of my past life no matter how hard I tried. I was convinced that the pipe was the only friend I needed, and the only cure to my misery.

PART 3

CHAPTER 1

AFTER A LONG BATTLE WITH DRUGS in my old neighborhood, I ended up moving to Memphis to care for my father. He had recently had a heart attack, and his health was failing, and two years later my mom died from a massive heart attack.

I blamed myself for my mothers death. I could only think of all the sleepless nights she had worrying about me. I was her baby boy, and I had failed at life tremendously. The day they lowered my mother's body in the ground was the most painful thing I'd ever experienced.

I stayed with him for nine years, in which, I spent three of them getting high, and in and out of prison. During my last three year sentence, he suffered a brain stroke, and passed away while I was incarcerated.

Three weeks later I was released without parole. I left Memphis and returned home, back to the same mess I'd left behind. I moved in with my nephew and his wife for a while, until my old habits resumed. My father had made me the beneficiary of his insurance policy, and my sister mailed me the check. As soon as the money hit my hands, the nightmare started all over again.

But, this time I had a legitimate excuse to use, and somehow my addiction seemed to know that. The death of my mom sent my life spiraling drastically outta control. Addiction had its way of geographically moving me around, and leading me into unfamiliar territory.

It wasn't until I ventured out in my new surroundings, that I found out it was much more to my habit than smoking. I was addicted to everything that came with the lifestyle. Hustling for the money, buying the product, gathering the paraphernalia, cooking it, and watching the glass pipe cloud up; I was addicted to it all.

I had burned every bridge, worn out every welcome, and let down everybody that ever trusted me. It was me against the world, and everything that came with it.

The new area wasn't that much of a difference from the other places my addiction lead me to. It was an open market for those who sold the poison, and those who abused it. Actually, it was worse than any part of the city I'd gotten high in. It wasn't a run down neighborhood, but, the evidence of hopelessness was all around for the eye to see.

The alleys were littered with used syringes, indicating the presence of heroin addicts, and those who chose to inject the cocaine instead of smoking it. I had never tried heroin because of my fear of needles, and the sickness I seen them go through when they couldn't get a fix.

Within a month of using, I found myself homeless again, sleeping in hallways, and abandoned buildings. Working for drug dealers to support my habit, not knowing they waited for me to make one mistake so they could make an example outta me.

I had my brief times of sobriety, but, they never lasted long. Getting clean, for me wasn't that hard to do, it was staying clean, I couldn't be consistent with. I couldn't shake that desire for that feeling no matter how hard I tried, and the more I thought about my mother, the more I wanted to be high.

I spent the next six years in and out of jail, and every incarceration was centered around my addiction in one way or another. I had attempted suicide twice, and ended up in a mental institution. I was at my lowest, eating outta garbage cans, and living on the streets. I was sick and tired of being sick and tired. The three ends of addiction were jails, institutions, and death; I'd seen two, jails and institutions, death was the only thing left.

It was a bitter cold winter night when I heard the voice of God. I was standing in front of the food and liquor store, about two o'clock in the morning. It was bitter cold, and the snow mixed with rain, pounded the small parking lot in front of the store. It was my last chance to hustle up on the money I needed to get high. My hands, and feet were numb and wet from the blistering mixture. I was at my breaking point, and enough was enough.

Right where I stood, I raised my hands above my head, and said, "God, if you will help me now, and sober me up, I will never touch it again, I'm tired Lord." And within a twinkling of an eye, I felt something move in me. I wasn't sure what I felt, but, I knew he had heard me. I could hear him saying, " trust me, and I will give you rest." The cravings, and the urges left my body and mind as if they were never there. It was a short conversation with God, but, the power he displayed was life changing for me. For the first time in my life, I felt like I knew him, and I belonged to him. He had lifted me up outta the fire, and placed me on solid ground.

I walked away from that horrible life that winter morning, December 29th, 2009. It was the day I got my sanity back. God had rescued me from the rest of me. He had given me the opportunity to change my circumstances, and I took it.

Two years later I enrolled in the Men's Bible Program. Instantly, I fell in love with the word of God. Surrounded by pastors everyday, I learned how to study God's word. I attended class three times a day, and worship service every day for eight months.

To my surprise, the school was filled with men and women who had traveled those same roads I had. Each Saturday, we shared our testimonies with one another. We were a family of individuals who had been beaten and defeated by the horrors of addiction. We had been to hell in back so many times, until there was no fight left in us.

God's grace and mercy had brought me outta the darkness, and into the light. I don't have to confine myself in shame and self-pity anymore, I am a living testimony of what God can do, only when you let go, and let him.

Today I am clean and sober. I wake up each morning with a praise in my heart, thanking God for his marvelous work in my life. Today I am persuaded that, neither height, nor depth, nor any other creature, shall be able to separate me from the love of God, which is in Christ Jesus our Lord.

It was that whisper in the wind I heard that cold winter morning, and I knew I would never have to ask God again, "CAN YOU HEAR ME NOW."

www.ingramcontent.com/pod-product-compliance
Lightning Source LLC
Chambersburg PA
CBHW021428070526
44577CB00001B/116